Derbyshire

A Journey of Discovery

By

Jon Millhouse

ShieldCrest

ISBN: 978-1-915657-88-6

MMXXIV

A CIP catalogue record for this is available from the British Library

Published by
ShieldCrest Publishing,
Boston, Lincs, PE20 3BT England
Tel: +44 (0) 333 8000 890
www.shieldcrest.co.uk

For Uncle Tony, in loving memory.
With thanks to Kimberley, Mum and Dad,
for your support in preparing this book.

Contents

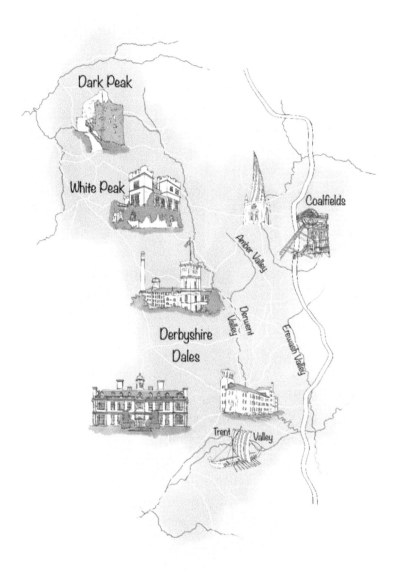

Derbyshire County Map

Courtesy Ethan Gill

Prologue

The idea first came to me during the Covid-19 lockdown of 2021. Five of us cooped up in our 3 bedroomed house, we were starting to climb the walls. We needed to exercise the kids' legs and my curious mind. We had to get out; we needed a change of scenery. Government restrictions dictated that we were only permitted to travel within the local area for outdoor exercise, which meant that our usual Sunday trips out were off limits. I therefore had to think creatively. Armed only with an Ordnance Survey map, I set about the unpromising task of trying to identify new and interesting places to explore within a 5-mile radius of home.

To my pleasant surprise completing this task not only proved to be possible, but something of a revelation. We enjoyed picnics and family walks at local beauty spots. I embarked on runs from home to seek out footpaths I hadn't explored before. Granted, after 6 weeks at home my first walk through a field felt like a stroll through the garden of Eden, but it was more than just the novelty of getting outside. We managed to find new vantage points and squeeze out new experiences from an impossibly small geographical area.

Hardly surprising if you think about it. England is so well trodden, so small and densely populated, so varied and has seen so much history, that it is possible to capture a rich tapestry of experiences in a single walk. I can leave my home and in the course of a single day encounter a Roman road, a Norman Castle, a Medieval Manor House, uplands, lowlands, wetlands, ordinary folk and members of the aristocracy. And this being England, four seasons of weather to boot. I doubt there is anywhere else on earth where this is the case, and we are blessed in this country with one of the most intricate and extensive footpath networks in the world – the fortunate coincidence of an historical compromise between the rights of the common folk to roam the countryside, and the desire of landowners to enclose it. Derbyshire alone has over 3,000 miles of public footpaths. I would challenge anybody to walk every inch of this extensive network.

I also began to realise that the experience of visiting a place – even one which is local and familiar – is so much richer if you are prepared to delve a little bit deeper into why it looks the way it does. Why the buildings have been designed in a particular way, how the landscape has been manipulated, who and what has gone before. In short, you get out what you put in. Nothing is interesting if you are not interested - but be curious, and there is so much to enjoy.

It is not just a matter of better appreciating the familiar. It is easy to assume that you know a place intimately when in fact, you don't. If we are being honest how much of our impression of a place is based upon the vantage point of travelling the same old roads, or visiting the same old places? We can live in a place for years and yet there are almost certainly backroads and footpaths within a few miles of home which we have never explored, and probably never will, unless we actively seek them out. Make the effort to do this and we will encounter interesting buildings we never knew existed, and new perspectives of familiar landscapes.

And there it was. The realisation that it was possible to explore and discover without actually travelling very far. Imagine if I broadened my search area out to the entirety of my home county. The possibilities were endless. And so, a plan was formed. Explore the length and breadth of Derbyshire, seeking out the people, places and issues which interest me. Ok, I have to admit, it was hardly the most ambitious or adventurous trip ever embarked upon, but that's beside the point. The point is that there is so much to be found close by.

In the modern era, the availability of cheap travel and the constant streaming of exotic images of far-flung places on our TVs and computer screens has seduced us into thinking that the only places worth exploring are elsewhere. The Georgians compiled a list of the 'ten wonders of the Peaks'. The Victorians waxed lyrical about the picturesque qualities of the Derbyshire Dales. We however have become indifferent about what is on our doorstep. Why mess about with Mam Tor when you can catch a short flight to the French Alps and marvel at Mont Blanc? It's hard to get excited about visiting Grindleford when you've been staring at a picture of the Grand Canyon all day on your computer home screen! But a place doesn't always have to be the biggest, the highest or the deepest to be worth visiting.

I had no desire to shrink my horizons, or those of my family. I love to travel, but visiting far flung places is not always possible, and may become less so in the future as we grapple with the challenges of increasing energy costs and climate change. The experience of exploring my locality during lockdown taught me that appreciation of a place is personal, subjective and changeable.

Nor did I wish to exist in a bubble, pretending that the only things which matter in the world are those which happen in our little piece of it. Quite the opposite in fact. I wanted to teach my kids – if I could tear them away from their electronic devices for more than 5 minutes – that you don't have to travel far to engage with big issues (past, present or future), and that context is everything. The way we live - our cultural differences, our idiosyncrasies – are all shaped by the way we interact with the outside world.

Derbyshire is a varied county, both geographically and socially. It is situated right in the middle of England, straddling its geophysical and socio-economic divides. It is where gentle lowlands meet rugged uplands. Red brick terraces coexist with country mansions, gritty working class communities rub shoulders with members of the aristocracy. It is a rich palimpsest of history, having played host to Roman legions, Medieval Kings and Viking invaders. In many ways, this county of contrasts is a microcosm of England itself. Like England therefore, its history is multi-layered and it's connections far reaching.

I therefore resolved to set off and explore my home county; often with unwitting family members, sometimes on my own. Predominantly using the back lanes rather than the better-known routes. Seeking out the forgotten corners instead of gravitating to the visitor hotspots. Where possible exploring places on foot rather than on motorised transport in order that I could properly connect with the environment around me.

What follows is an account of these meanderings through Derbyshire, recounting some of its long history in (roughly) chronological order, describing its varied places, observing its quirky communities and considering some of the issues they face. Above all else, I talk about things that interest me through the prism of one County.

CHAPTER 1

Nobles and Norsemen
The Trent Valley

"A great heathen force came into English Land."
(The Anglo-Saxon Chronicle)

We launched our vessel onto the mighty River Trent dodging rocks and eddies amidst an ancient awe-inspiring landscape where Viking armies had once camped and ancient Britons had traded. At least, that was how the experience seemed in my imagination. In reality we were drifting at a snails pace past an industrial estate in Burton upon Trent; bemused anglers looking on. I had picked up my brother an hour earlier – tired and hungover- and driven us to the launch spot for an organised canoe trip. One of those birthday presents where I had bought him something that I actually wanted to do myself. We were 1 of 5 canoes left to paddle 10 miles or so downstream on our own.

The weather was unseasonably hot and dry, the water low and benign. Every so often Pete and I would paddle frantically towards what looked like a turbulent patch of water in search of an adrenaline kick, only to receive momentary acceleration. The organisers' warnings about the canoes possibly capsizing seemed rather unnecessary. I struggled to see how that was possible in these conditions. Until, that is, I saw another of the party dripping wet and complaining of capsizing within seconds of embarkation. White knuckle it may not have been but tranquil and relaxing it most definitely was. We soon cleared the urban sprawl of Burton and were out into the countryside. The low water level meant that our view of the surrounding countryside was restricted by the high river banks. Swallows darted playfully beside the riverside vegetation. Dragonflies hovered above the water. Cows came down from an adjoining field for a drink and I saw my first heron. It is amazing how rural and tranquil even this crowded part of England - with its electricity pylons, factories and power stations – can seem.

We soon approached the Staffordshire/Derbyshire border. Or at least, I think we did. There was no sign post, checkpoint or fanfare. Why would there be? The border is of no consequence really. Well I think it ought to be.

Derbyshire has existed as a county for around 1000 years, with its borders roughly the same as they are today. It is significantly older than most nation states. Germany and Italy weren't unified until 1871.

The continental U.S.A didn't reach its full extent until 1845 – and even then proceeded to split in two a few years later. Many countries in the Middle East and Africa have borders which are arrow-straight, having been drawn arbitrarily by colonial administrators at the beginning of the twentieth century (often with tragic long-lasting consequences). I guess borders – in an accurate "line on a map" sense - are a fairly modern construct, rather like the concept of land ownership. For most of human history there must have been 'peoples' and 'territories' – defined by natural geographical features.

Historians believe that in the centuries following the collapse of Roman rule in Britain, small fiefdoms grew up, geographically defined by rivers. What little evidence does exist of the so-called dark ages suggest a series of names for these communities – several of which survive as the names of rivers. These small territories eventually amalgamated into larger kingdoms - Southern Derbyshire being part of the kingdom of Mercia. "Merce" means "borderland" in old Mercian dialect.

I can't help but think that the Trent – a significant natural barrier, even more so in the medieval period – must have formed a frontier at some stage. It must have been a scene of conflict, particularly when Scandinavian Invaders were marauding around these parts in the 9th Century. The treaty of Wedmore between Alfred of Wessex and the Viking King

Guthrum eventually saw the establishment of Danish rule north and east of a line between London and Chester – not far from the route of the Trent. Prior to this in 873 the Viking Great army crossed the Trent and established a camp at Repton, the subject of a recent archaeological discovery.

And so our regional differences, our cultural identities, have been shaped by this as much as anything else. The Trent Valley has as good a claim as any as England's fabled north south divide in my view, separating as it does the rugged uplands, industrial towns and coalfields to the North, from the gentle, pastoral lowlands to the South. Wealth has always tended to flow downhill, as if influenced by gravity. If Derbyshire's Trent Valley historically marked the approximate border between the cultured Mercians and Kingdom of Wessex to the South and West, and the rough arsed Vikings to the North and East, little wonder that there survives such a pronounced difference in accents, dialects and identity, one side of that line to the other.

We were getting into the groove and proceeding at what I thought was a reasonable pace. Until that is, 3 teenage lads on the canoe behind us came tearing past, leaving us feeling rather embarrassed. They did in fairness have a numerical advantage and age on their side, but their insistence on playing music loudly on a mobile phone – a mix of 1980's pop music oddly enough – shattered the tranquillity of the scene and irritated me greatly.

After passing the village of Newton Solney, which appeared almost French somehow with its chateau-like riverside stone buildings framed by wooded slopes and shimmering in the afternoon haze, we approached Repton and the area of the riverbank where the Vikings had camped. The site is now a peaceful cornfield, but in the winter of 873/4 it must have been a forbidding sight. The 'Great Heathen Army', a coalition of Scandinavian warriors, invaded England in 865. In 873, they decided to have a crack at Repton, then the site of a wealthy monastery and capital of the kingdom of Mercia. After over wintering at this very riverbank they disposed of the Mercian King Burgned and installed Viking King Ceolwulf in his place. The subsequent peace treaty of 878 saw the establishment of Danish rule across the East Midlands, which persisted until the 11th Century.

The Scandinavian influence survives amongst all of us who hail from these parts, and I don't just mean flat pack furniture and meatballs. Place names such as those ending in 'by' or 'thorpe', words such as 'window' and 'egg', a few choice swear words and a flat accent. Above all else, it is in our blood. I was surprised to discover upon taking ancestry DNA tests a couple of years ago that I am apparently 12%

Scandinavian. Mind you, it has been suggested that Britain's various waves of invaders did not leave as strong a DNA footprint as you might think. Historian Michael Wood claims that of those who can trace their family history to Britain pre-1945, two thirds of their DNA is pre-Roman Britannic. The exception to this rule? You guessed it – a path between Norfolk and the Trent Valley, where Britannic DNA is apparently much lower suggesting a comprehensive population replacement by those pesky Vikings.

The Danish Vikings certainly had a fondness for Repton. The curiously named Viking King 'Ivar the Boneless' (who was apparently 9ft tall), is said to have been found buried in St Wystan's churchyard by a farm labourer in 1686. It is perhaps not surprising that the Vikings were drawn to the Trent Valley. They were after all famed for their 'riverine empires', penetrating deep into Continental Europe via navigable rivers upon their long boats. The Trent offered access by boat from the North Sea to Central England. If Repton was also at that time a centre of power and riches, little wonder the Norsemen were drawn to the town like moths to a flame. Archaeologists have found Mercian coins dating from the 9th Century as far away as North East Scotland. The Scandinavians, rather than the Mercians, were likely responsible for their redistribution – probably via the River Trent.

Rivers Matter: I am one of those sad people who take an interest (if only momentarily) in the motorway signs which proclaim the passing of a river. I suspect that I am in the minority. I dare say that the majority of people take far more notice of the motorway signs which promise a service station with a Burger King, Costa or M&S. For unless your home happens to have been flooded recently, rivers are for most people nowadays, of little or no consequence.

But rivers do matter. For millennia they have been vital to human existence. Providing water for drinking, cleaning, raising livestock and watering crops. Powering mills and supplying industries. Facilitating the movement of people and goods. Defining boundaries and providing defensible frontiers. Enabling invasion. Sculpting and nourishing the land to enable crop cultivation and therefore human settlement. Powering the industries that followed. It is no coincidence that nearly all of our major urban conurbations are centred on or around rivers.

I am a strong believer in the theory that geography can be determinative. In his book 'Prisoners of Geography' Tim Marshall convincingly argues that global politics is inextricably linked to

Geography. That the behaviour and psyche of populations across the world is determined by their physical environment. Others have similarly suggested that the northern coast of the Mediterranean basin was a cradle of ancient civilisation because of its craggy coves, lumps and bumps which facilitated a maritime culture. Applying the same principles, but at a smaller scale, the rivers of England can be said to have determined who lives where and how they live.

A little while later, after a picnic stop on a gravel bar, we rounded the bend to see the teenagers up ahead mucking about and sustaining little speed. My competitive spirit kicked in. This was our opportunity to restore some pride. Like an Oxford boat race coxswain I barked orders at Pete – row, row, row – I don't care if you were up till 4 in the morning last night - row! The plan worked. We were much quicker when paddling in unison and the teenagers were disadvantaged by their hijinks. We steamed past with the sound of George Michael's Careless Whisper ringing in our ears.

Keen to maintain our advantage I badgered Pete into keeping up a good tempo. We rounded several more bends and sailed past the rotting hulk of the disused Willington Power station cooling towers – a monument to brutalist 20th century engineering – and finally, the finish line. A great way to travel, I have to admit, at least when travelling downstream.

I returned to Repton on another day, this time accompanied by Kimberley and our 4 year old daughter, Annie. We found Repton to be a sleepy place – a prestigious private school super imposed on a quiet village. Save for a few well dressed and equally well-spoken teenagers walking between classes, and a couple of teachers walking along clutching text books, the streets were empty – and this despite us visiting on a Friday. No wonder Jeremy Clarkson, who went to school at Repton, wrote of being bored at the place. It wasn't always like this however. It is hard to imagine now but Repton was once the epicentre of central England, being as it was the capital of the medieval Kingdom of Mercia.

Mercia was founded in 527 by Anglo Saxon King Icel. One of several medieval kingdoms in the British Isles, Repton became its capital in the 7th century, there being a monastery in the town after 653. Mercia had its heyday between the years 600 and 900 and is best remembered today for King Offas Dyke along the Welsh border. In 1170 an Augustinian Priory was established and then in 1557, Repton College. The college was established for the local poor, which is ironic given that the institution is today one of the most exclusive private schools in England. As well as Messr. Clarkson, famous alumni at Repton also included Roald Dahl and not one, but two Archbishops of Canterbury.

The Mercians were so powerful in their day that they conquered and ruled London for a time and constructed a 169 mile partition along the Welsh Border. It is strange to think of Midlanders ruling the roost – like having Jasper Carrott as Prime Minister and Lenny Henry as Chancellor of the Exchequer. In all seriousness this was a proper Kingdom which existed for centuries, and given that Repton was its capital for a time it would have been a place of real importance and prestige. One of the most striking characters of the age was Æthelflæd 'the lady of the Mercians', inspiration for JRR Tolkien's Lord of the Rings character Éowyn the shieldmaiden of Rohan. Eldest daughter of Alfred the great, Æthelflæd led Mercia in battle against the Danes, and became the first British queen to singlehandedly rule a Kingdom. In 917 her army recaptured Derby from the Danes. Why is there no statue of her in Derby? Bonnie Prince Charlie is commemorated with a statue behind Derby Cathedral for riding into town with his Jacobite Army in 1745 and signing a piece of paper confirming his surrender. Æthelflæd is the kind of character I want my daughter to grow up talking about.

Passing the 'Hogwarts-esque' school buildings and medieval stone arch we approached St. Wystons Church, with its tall perpendicular spire and spacious churchyard. We entered the church and admired the grand interior; the only people present in the building. In the corner were a set of steps descending into the room I had come to see; the famous (or perhaps not so famous judging by the complete absence of any other visitors) Anglo-Saxon Crypt. While Kimberley entertained Annie, pretending the pews were benches on a bus, I walked down to the Crypt. It was fascinating, eerie and atmospheric. It was smaller than I anticipated, but this just added a sense of intimacy. Constructed in the first half of the 8th century the Crypt was the final resting place of Mercian Kings Æthelbald and Wiglaf (757 and 840) as well as the latter's Grandson (849). Remarkably the Crypt was 'lost' after the 16th century and only discovered by chance when a workman digging a hole for a grave broke through the ceiling and fell into it in 1779. Although a little rough around the edges (anything would be after 1,300 years), the architecture was clearly sophisticated and impressive. Carved rounded stone columns held up vaulted ceilings. Small windows let in a tiny amount of light.

It blows my mind to think that this small room was the spiritual and cultural centre of a Kingdom – and not just an insignificant provincial community – but a Kingdom which existed for centuries and which was so powerful at its height that it ruled the whole of the Midlands and beyond. And to think that this room was forgotten about and only accidentally found again! I must confess I did feel a little like Indiana Jones. Save for the low-level electric lighting and a few medieval modifications, the scene was essentially as it must have been a thousand years earlier. The fact that I was underneath the main church, unable to see the outside world, further added to the time travelling vibe. I wouldn't have been surprised to climb back up the steps and find myself in the year 900.

Looking for somewhere to have lunch we carried on to the aptly-named Mercia Marina. After Repton this proved to be quite a peculiar sight – quintessential English narrowboats juxtaposed with strikingly modern buildings housing boutique shops, all set within the South Derbyshire countryside which is about as far as it is possible to get from the sea in England. Upon arrival we immediately dived into a popular looking café. Every table inside and out was taken bar one, quite a shock after the emptiness of Repton. Clearly the combination of frothy coffees, inexpensive paninis and a view over narrowboats floating in a flooded gravel pit was too irresistible for the hoards of retirees who had descended on the establishment this lunchtime.

After the splendour of Repton I quickly lowered the level of cultural sophistication by ordering fried egg, chips and beans and hoped that Kimberley wouldn't be tempted to buy any of the over-priced knick-knacks which I knew would inevitably be offered for sale in the incongruously sited shops across the Marina (a wish that proved to be futile).

We continued eastward along the Trent and Mersey Canal towpath, which roughly follows the route of the River Trent. A pleasant walk, the scene was essentially rural, with a few residential settlements visible. And yet, we could see in the distance the chimneys of the enormous Toyota car factory and hear the rumble of cars travelling along the A50. Strange place; South Derbyshire. Rural and built up all at the same time. Modern, but also ancient. A place which to most people doesn't matter, that is anonymous. The no-mans land between 3 cities (Derby, Nottingham and Leicester) in the middle of England, that thousands of people whizz past every day en-route to somewhere more important. Even the name of 'East Midlands' Airport is depressingly anonymous. It is Derbyshire's equivalent of that bit of concrete wasteland you find beneath motorway flyovers. And yet, it feels like it should matter, and that it would have mattered in the past. The confluence of 2 important rivers which have brought trade, industry, transport, flat fertile soils and a natural defensible barrier.

No place illustrates these conditions more so than Swarkestone Bridge. At three quarters of a mile long, this medieval structure is the longest stone bridge in England, and was the principal crossing point along the River Trent for centuries. It remains magnificent, in both scale and antiquity – dominating the broad flood plain below. But from a modern, practical sense, it simply gets in the way. The actual crossing of the river is achieved via a relatively narrow humpback bridge; the majority of the length of the structure comprises of a raised causeway which no doubt once transversed marshy, boggy ground but today simply sits above well drained fields. There is an almost constant stream of two-way traffic, including, for some reason buses and lorries ill suited to the various narrow pinch points along it's length. This affords the crossing of the bridge a sense of jeopardy, as you hope you don't encounter a wide vehicle travelling in the opposite direction at the wrong moment.

Not far from Swarkestone bridge is Swarkestone Hall pavilion, a 17th century Jacobean style folly of unknown purpose sitting sentinel-like in this flat, green landscape. Resembling a hunting lodge – come Tudor country house in miniature, this elegant and symmetrical stone structure with its oddly oriental looking cupolas is evocative of the monumental history and importance of this landscape. Yet its purpose in the modern age seems to have been reduced to the backdrop for a famous Rolling Stones album cover (with Mick Jagger and Keith Richards et al casually sprawled across its magnificent mullioned windows), and an upmarket holiday cottage. It strikes me that England is gradually turning into a giant heritage-based theme park.

Speaking of heritage-based theme parks, our final stop on this particular leg of my journey was the small historic market town of Melbourne. We discovered a curving high street containing a dense cluster of traditional buildings of all shapes and sizes hosting cafes, delicatessens and expensive looking estate agents. Melbourne appeared to be thriving, and a popular place to live for those who value that intangible quality that historic towns possess - character. On the outskirts of town we passed a couple of new build housing estates which curiously had sought to capitalise on this demand for all things old by attempting to replicate an historic built environment. One in particular had really gone to town, even to the extent of incorporating a faux market place. It was most bizarre -a 21st century development pretending to be an 18th century village - but certainly more aesthetically pleasing than most modern housing developments. This was doubtless following the example set by Poundbury in Dorset - an unashamed modern replica of a traditional town championed by the then Prince of Wales but loathed by many architects for being 'artificial'. It says a lot about our national psyche that many of us yearn to live in a place which looks like it is 1890. But without the cholera, horse muck and coal dust. And with electric cars, Wi-Fi and Netflix. How odd.

South of the town centre was a group of historic buildings which certainly didn't lack authenticity, including Melbourne Hall and Saint Michael and Saint Mary's church. This part of town oozed historic character and ambience. The yards and outbuildings to the rear of the hall had been reused to host a bar, cafe and a few shops. Everything looked old, but the place had plenty of life and activity. It reminded me of my time living in Oxford. The hall overlooked an attractive walled garden and its setting was further enhanced by the adjacent lake, which looked resplendent twinkling in the spring sunshine. To the west of the hall was the church, a grand looking edifice with a stout looking castellated Norman tower at one end. The interior was quite something. Double storey arched stone columns all the way down the nave, which conjured images in my mind of a crusader state castle or medieval cathedral in Granada or Sicily. I wondered if this is what inspired Melbourne's most famous son, Thomas Cook, to develop his pioneering package holidays to the continent.

Thomas Cook actually came from more humble beginnings. His modest home was demolished many years ago, but before leaving Melbourne we visited the Baptist church where he had preached. A grand building in its own way, but certainly not containing the extravagance of Saint Michael and Saint Mary's church. Cook established a travel agency which provided the burgeoning Victorian middle classes with all-inclusive grand tours of Germany, France, Italy and even cruises down the Nile. In doing so he effectively established mass tourism and popularized package holidays. He and his wife however were strong advocates of the temperance movement. I wonder what they would have made of some of today's booze-fuelled package holidays.

In the spirit of Thomas Cook's yearning for travel it was time to move on to the next leg of my journey. Sadly, the Erewash Valley does not have the lustre of the Nile Valley, but I was sure I would find plenty of interesting sights to explore.

CHAPTER 2

Power and Protest – The Amber and Erewash Valleys

"This was the pith of England…."
(Author D.H. Lawrence describing the Erewash Valley)

I could see the outskirts of Ilkeston on the horizon to the east and the Derby suburb of Spondon lay only a few miles to the west, but no matter, the scene before us was timeless. For we were walking along the route of the Portway, that most ancient of pathways which carried travellers the length and breadth of Derbyshire for hundreds, if not thousands of years. And what is more we were at Dale Abbey, the site of a medieval monastery and hermitage. The steps of ancient travellers could almost be heard echoing through time.

Stretching diagonally across Derbyshire over a distance of 48 miles from the river ports in the south-east to the Celtic hill fort of Mam Tor in the north-west, was the ancient trackway known as the 'Portway'. Thought to be over 2,000 years old, the route was 'rediscovered' in the 1930s.

It seemed rather apt to begin my tracing of the Portway at Dale Abbey; Kimberley the children and I out for a winter walk. First past the hermit's cave said to have been carved out of rock at the beginning of the 12th century by a Derby baker, fleeing to this valley for a life of solitary prayer. Perhaps Derby County were in a bad run of form. There is something compelling about caves that used to be lived in by people - they make popular tourist attractions the world over. My kids certainly thought so. They couldn't wait to scramble up to the cave and poke their heads through the windows. On past the tiny All Saints Church, the smallest Parish Church in the county, created from a remnant of the old monastery. And finally, the Abbey itself, or at least what's left of it, namely a single, albeit tall and elegant, stone archway. Fountains Abbey this isn't, but nonetheless when the low winter sun shines through the arch as it did on this day, the scene is evocative and timeless. For in its day this was a building of splendour and importance.

Founded around 1200, all that remains of the main abbey building is the frame of what would have been an awe-inspiring 40-foot window.

The Abbey is by no means the biggest of its type, but it is representative of the power and wealth enjoyed by religious institutions in medieval England. Prior to the dissolution of the monasteries and the seizing of their lands by Henry VIII in the 16th century, the church owned about a third of all the productive land in England, and by extension, a third of the peasant workforce and a third of the fighting men - in those days higher class 'knights' who were called to arms for campaigns in France and the crusades in the Holy Land.

The route of the Portway continues from Dale Abbey in a north-westerly direction past the villages of Stanley and Morley, along the Centenary/Midshires Way. This well-preserved piece of countryside just a stone's throw from Derby contains all of the classic landscape features which tell the story of how rural England has been manipulated and controlled for the past millennia. The tell-tale ridges and furrows preserved in fields, which were created by medieval farmers walking their oxen and ploughs up and down what were then big, open, communal fields for growing crops; the 'moors' and 'commons' where ordinary folk were allowed to graze their animals; the woodlands where they could collect fire wood; the 'tithe' barn at Morley where local people were expected to bring a proportion of their produce as taxation; the impressive 11th century church next door, which looked after the spiritual health of a god-fearing population; the remnants of old manor houses and priories.

The lords of the manor nominally owned the land, but crucially, local people had rights to plough a 'furlong' or two in the communal field, to graze on the commons, and to take wood from the trees. This all changed from the 17th century onwards, when successive 'enclosure' acts in Parliament resulted in the outright ownership and fencing off of land, here and everywhere else in the country, by the better off in society. On the one hand this resulted in much more efficient forms of agriculture, the 'improvement' of fallow land, and an opportunity for a few of the more enterprising common folk to improve themselves. On the other hand, those who were left behind could be left disenfranchised and destitute. An owner could now do what he wanted with his land, even if that meant kicking off the peasants and replacing them with sheep. This eventually contributed to the mass exodus of the rural population into industrial towns in the 18th and 19th centuries.

And this landscape has been preserved to tell its story in no small part due to a modern form of manipulation and control; it is part of the Nottingham-Derby Greenbelt. The Greenbelt is a planning policy tool initiated after the second world war to protect a 'doughnut' of countryside around many towns and cities from most forms of development. With development having been stifled for decades in the very locations where it was most likely to happen, the policy has resulted in a sort of 'parallel universe'. Prettier parts of the Greenbelt have become enclaves for better off commuters – an opportunity to live the rural idyll within 10 minutes of the office. Conversely, scruffier sections have been left unimproved for decades; grazed by a few horses perhaps but otherwise devoid of meaningful agriculture or industry, and prevented from being recreational or biodiversity resources by the private ownership of landlords content to sit on the land for years in the hope that they may one day be able to sell it at a huge profit to build houses.

Critics of Greenbelt policy argue that it has negative social and economic consequences; stifling economic growth, leaving settlements which are remote from major towns isolated, and forcing the majority of the population to cram together in cities, competing for a limited, ageing and evermore expensive housing stock. Personally, I believe that the benefits outweigh the negative consequences. Just imagine the alternative in a landscape such as this one: inevitable urban sprawl; settlements merging into one another; Derby city centre largely abandoned in favour of edge of town commercial districts and all of those age-old landscape features I talked about earlier, gone forever.

I do believe that there is a big missed opportunity in the way that Greenbelt land is used however. Just imagine how much of a tremendous resource it would be for our urban populations if all green belt land was turned over tomorrow to public recreation, growing food for the local community and creating a haven for wildlife. I would suggest that the physical and mental wellbeing of much of the population would improve markedly. The trouble is of course that unless the Government intends to buy up vast tracts of land at great expense, such a policy would fly in the face of that most English of rights – the right of private land ownership. Something which manifested itself most forcibly after the enclosure acts but which had its roots, as we shall see later in this chapter, in the Norman Conquest of 1000 years ago.

I reached Morley, the scene of one of the first of many acts of rebellion over the years in this restless corner of Derbyshire. In 1381, the year of the 'Great Rebellion' in London, a wealthy woman from Morley by the name of Goditha de Stathum, together with her five sons, decided to get in on the action. Two of her sons, William and Richard, went on a killing spree before setting fire to Breadsall Priory and then taking Horsley Castle by force and hoisting a flag atop its tower to announce their attempted takeover. The insurrection didn't achieve very much and Goditha harboured her sons together with accomplices until they were eventually put on trial. Goditha must have been a shrewd political operator as all five sons were eventually pardoned, some of them ending up in the army fighting at Agincourt. Goditha, perhaps in an effort to atone for her family's sins, went on to fund rebuilding works at Morley Church.

I continued on to Breadsall Priory, a 13th century Augustinian Priory-come-Elizabethan Manor House; once the home of Erasmus Darwin (18th century physician, philosopher, inventor and all-round clever clogs) and now a fancy golf club. The manicured splendour, neatly-cut grass and antiquated buildings nestled amongst rolling mist-covered hills and gnarled old trees had a feeling of timelessness and orderliness, appropriate for an old priory. The comings and goings of Audis, BMWs and Teslas along the main drive did rather jar with the scene.

I continued in a north-westerly direction. I couldn't resist visiting the remains of Horsley Castle, once a 12th century royal military tower, sitting forgotten on a wooded hillside overlooking the A38. Thousands of motorists speed past daily unaware of its existence.

At Coxbench, the route of the Portway veered northwards towards Holbrook, along a road still called 'Portway', but I continued westward along the Midshires Way long distance footpath. After crossing some farmland, the path abruptly descended into the

Derwent Valley at Edgehill, squeezing between some houses perched on the hillside before revealing a pleasant vista of the valley plain and the village of Duffield beyond. All along the eastern valley side - along Eaton Bank to my left and Duffield Bank to my right - were scattered fine houses, both old and new, interspersed with trees and old stone quarries. The millionaires' row of the northern Derby fringes. After reaching the valley bottom and crossing a humped stone bridge, I approached Duffield, a large, elegant village occupying the lower westerly slopes of the Derwent Valley beside an expansive flat meadow and an impressive looking stone church, which resembled a miniature cathedral. Everything in Duffield has a sense of quality and above all, confidence. After passing along the high street with its boutique shops and eateries - no bargain basement establishments here - I reached what is perhaps the root of this self-assurance - Duffield Castle.

As I approached the innocuous gated entrance at the base of the motte (mound), a National Trust sign advised me to 'bring my imagination'. I'd certainly need it, because the castle here was demolished in 1071, punishment for its owner William de Ferrers joining a failed rebellion against Henry II. This was an early example of rebellion in this part of Derbyshire – something which proved to be a recurring theme over the subsequent centuries. The de Ferrers family were at it again in 1266 when

William's descendant Robert joined another failed rebellion against King Henry III. I climbed a set of steps, flanked by metal railings adorned with clever inscriptions evoking the spirit of the place, before emerging onto the top of the mound. All that is left of the castle itself are the stone foundations, but gazing out over the surrounding valley and "using my imagination" it was possible to connect with the history of the place. I often prefer to have to use my imagination at such historical monuments. I always think that Windsor Castle is too complete, in too pristine a condition. There is something evocative about a romantic ruin.

The green valley below seemed very civilised somehow – a wild landscape tamed. That's what Norman castles were all about. William the Conqueror's decision to reward his barons with huge estates and retain great swathes of land for himself as mere 'hunting forests' resulted in a power structure which had far reaching consequences.

The Norman invasion supplanted the English aristocracy with a new French-speaking elite; culturally distinct and emphasising a greater division between the ruling classes and the peasantry. Here were the roots of the class hierarchy which is an intrinsic part of our culture to the present day. William's cronies were given titles and land such as here at Duffield. It is surprising how many of the modern-day aristocracy can trace their roots back to the Normans. And with that land they built castles – to defend, to subdue and above all else to act as the ultimate status symbol. Little wonder the English country house became so popular in subsequent centuries and, as the phrase goes "the Englishman's home is his castle".

Let us not kid ourselves. These were shock and awe tactics by an invading force: the mass dispossession of land and its turning over to royal hunting forests such as the Duffield Frith; the granting of titles and power to prominent Norman knights such as de Ferrers; the systematic destruction of communities across the north of England in an effort to quell rebellion. The consequences for the incumbent population must have been catastrophic.

The Norman Conquest is a perfect example of where history turned on a quirk of fate. William was an upstart from Normandy with a tenuous claim to the English throne, (Edward the Confessor apparently promised it to him). Had England not been invaded a few weeks earlier by Norwegian king Harold Hardrada; had the English king Harold Godwinson not had to expend resources and men roundly defeating the Viking invader at the battle of Stamford Bridge near York; had he not chosen to immediately march his exhausted men to meet

William on the south coast, but bide his time, muster more troops and allow William to isolate himself; all could have been different. As it was, William defeated Harold at the Battle of Hastings and seized the English crown. In the months and years that followed a small gang of French pretenders were able to supplant a pre-existing ruling elite and impose their will on an entire population. And how did William achieve such subjugation? By dividing up great swathes of land amongst himself and his chums and building castles. The castle was the ultimate status symbol. Nothing says "we are in charge now and we're here to stay" like an impregnable mansion atop a large mound. Duffield had rather a large one - one of the largest in England in fact - with stone walls 15 feet thick and a massive private hunting forest to boot.

The concentration of so much power and land in the hands of a small band of Norman barons established a power structure which had ramifications throughout the following centuries. Tensions between the barons and the crown created a power struggle which ultimately led to the curtailing of the king's power in the form of the Magna Carta, that much celebrated bill of rights which established the rule of law as the ultimate arbitrator and not the monarch. It led to the establishment of a parliament and in turn, a parliamentary democracy. It resulted in a small but sufficiently numerous and sufficiently wealthy group of families who were able to invest in agricultural improvements, maritime trade, mills and factories, which in turn facilitated the industrial revolution and the expansion of empire. And perhaps most enduringly of all, it created a class system which is so ingrained in English society, no amount of "levelling up" projects by modern governments could truly destroy it.

As if echoing its distant past as a centre of baronial power and prestige, Duffield and the neighbouring villages of Quarndon and Hazelwood exist today as a focal point for local power and wealth. Derby's business owners, lawyers and professional footballers choose to live here, enjoying the rural setting, delicatessens and train line to London. The biggest draw of all however is the local secondary school. Traditionally acknowledged as the best state school in the county, aspirational parents clamour to live in the Ecclesbourne School catchment, paying a handsome premium to do so. Here we have a real-life example of what Daniel Markovits describes in his book of the same name 'The Meritocracy Trap', a new type of aristocracy based on access to high quality schooling – and the opportunities and social networks which follow.

I continued north along the A6, the old turnpike road which follows the path of the river Derwent. I could see the opposite valley-side liberally sprinkled with expensive properties set behind stone walls. I crossed the river at Milford, a picturesque former industrial village squeezed into a narrow stretch of the Derwent Valley. Here Jedediah Strutt constructed revolutionary 'fireproof' cotton mills with iron frames at the end of the 18th century (modern -day residents like to claim that Milford was, architecturally speaking, a forerunner to Manhattan. I'm fairly sure the residents of Manhattan don't share this sentiment). Strutt's stout, stone built workers cottages remain along with a handful of traditional pubs. Just south of Milford is the hamlet of Makeney, where it is possible to find the famous Holly Bush Inn. Dating from the late 17th century, the pub is allegedly a former haunt of highwayman Dick Turpin. Highwaymen were responsible for robbing unsuspecting travellers by the side of the road. Nowadays, motorway service stations perform the same function; albeit with less threat of violence. It's curious how much we celebrate ruthless criminals when we have the reassurance of three centuries of separation. I suspect the Dick Turpin connection has done no harm to the Holly Bush's popularity.

You might reasonably wonder why a highwayman was knocking about in Makeney, which receives about as much passing traffic these days as Timbuktu. The answer of course is that in Dick

Turpin's days (the early 18th century), it was situated on the main north-south road through the Derwent Valley. The A6 wasn't constructed until the beginning of the 19th century.

Continuing northwards the route is downgraded to a bridle path - rather like the Portway, a once important roadway now quiet but with echoes of the people who passed before. I passed Wildersley Farm. I once read an estate agents advert for the place which rather amusingly claimed that Elizabeth I had once travelled past the property. I reckon that if Elizabeth I and Dick Turpin had visited everywhere it is claimed they had been, they must have both lived until they were 200. Quite how anyone is supposed to verify these claims is beyond me!

Through Belper, a delightful, bustling former mill town, where the Strutt's really went to town building cotton mills, workers houses, schools, churches, even a swimming baths. A very early example of a complete industrial settlement – but more of that in a subsequent chapter. Today, Belper exists as one-half historic mill town, one-half enormous and monotonous 1990s housing estate. I'm not critical of this, I'm fairly certain the former wouldn't have enjoyed its recent renaissance without the injection of people and funds brought about by the latter. The textile industry was so dominant in Belper – an entire sizable town supported directly or indirectly for nearly two centuries – that it needed change quickly to avoid rapid decline.

North of Belper I reached Nether Heage. At a quiet crossroads on a hill overlooking the village were two reminders of power and conflict. A rather incongruously positioned factory owes its location to its previous use as a camp for Italian prisoners of war during the second world war. The extent of wartime infrastructure and personnel across the English countryside during the second world war is mindboggling. Military camps hastily imposed on sleepy villages. Southern England in particular resembled a giant barracks with two million American service personnel passing through alone. Worlds must have collided. Soldiers from far-flung lands suddenly living among provincial country folk. Perhaps the Italian POWs gazed over Nether Heage from their lofty vantage point on a summer's evening and the sight of the windmill, rolling hills and stone cottages reminded them of Tuscany. If they squinted. Perhaps they snook out on occasion and nipped down the hill to the Spanker for a glass of red wine. A few apparently stayed on after the war and settled down with local girls.

Slightly further along from the factory, set back off the road beside a footpath, was another monument to power and conflict; a surviving cold war bunker. The entrance shaft and air tunnel survive randomly in a field at a local high point affording views over both the Amber and Derwent valleys. At least in the case of a nuclear apocalypse, the view through the periscope would have been good. Once again, I was reminded of the potential for conflict, or in this case the threat of it, to manifest itself in such quiet, inconsequential places. We think of ourselves as separated from places where war is waged. Perhaps we are not quite so separate. Mind you, I struggle to see the effectiveness of such installations. During the height of the cold war, the USA and USSR had nuclear arsenals large enough to obliterate all of us. It's hard to believe that a couple of scout masters mucking around with a CB radio in a tiny concrete bunker outside Nether Heage would have made much difference.

Having holidayed in Normandy twice now and watched World War two aircraft swoop in formation across the allied landings beaches, the low rumble of their engines leaving a lump in my throat, I can understand the sense of pride and patriotism that is generated by memories of the last world war. Both my grandfathers served in the war and I am immensely moved by their stories. But I feel I have the perspective that the best part of a century brings to also understand that war is never one-dimensional. Those same aircraft wreaked havoc in Dresden. Pride and patriotism is all very well but we've all seen the ugly side of such sentiments in less scrupulous regimes and how powerful a tool it can be in the wrong hands.

The second world war cast a huge shadow over the remainder of the 20th century and having grown up at the tail end of that century, I believe my generation was the last to experience its lasting influence on popular culture. I am also amongst the last to have first-hand memories of grandparents who participated in the conflict. This link has now gone for subsequent generations. I suspect this is both good and bad.

War is that most enduring of by-products of civilisation. We might reasonably assume that the words 'civilised' and 'war' are mutually exclusive, yet ever since the human race began to organise itself into civilisations war has been a repeated scourge. I'm sure hunter gatherer peoples were capable of acts of spontaneous violence, but once we had organisation and centralisation as a society, we had the capabilities to wage war, and once our resources, land, food, and raw materials became property, we had the motivation to do so. Think of the archetypal 'civilised' society and we might think of ancient Athens or Rome with their sophisticated methods of governance – but war with 'outsiders' on the margins of empire was a constant characteristic of those ancient societies. Even here in Britain, where internal peace has been maintained for the past three centuries under a parliamentary democracy, war has been a constant preoccupation. During this time Britain has invaded, occupied, armed or liberated the majority of countries on earth. War, or the reminder of war, is never too far away. As if to illustrate this point, after passing through Nether Heage, with its stone cottages and windmill, and descending to Buckland Hollow, I passed through Valley Farm, who's owner adamantly assures me there are second world war Rolls Royce aeroplane engines buried under his farm buildings.

I carried on northwards, past some tranquil fishing ponds, over a redundant hump back bridge which used to straddle the Cromford Canal and an equally redundant former canal keepers house (now a pub), over the busy A610, into a field and I finally reached the River Amber.

The Amber is so small and inconsequential that if we were in North America it wouldn't warrant inclusion on the map, never mind be worthy of the name 'river' and yet it has seen so much history. Illustrating this point precisely I could see a few hundred metres upstream Amber Mill, where the famous 19th century engineer and inventor Joseph Whitworth served his apprenticeship, and up on the hill in the distance, the silhouette of Wingfield Manor. The scene was one of complete tranquillity. The River Amber slowly meandering through the landscape, rolling hills and occasional farms. No-one around and no sound, save for the occasional rumble of a tractor engine. This isn't spectacular countryside by any means. It isn't part of a national park or area of outstanding natural beauty. I could see a road and the edge of a town on the horizon. But no matter, it is a delightful and forgotten pocket of English countryside.

This area is part of Wingfield Park. It is a well-preserved remnant of the medieval hunting forest attached to Wingfield Manor. It's modest size and location next to the unassuming towns of Ripley and Alfreton mean that nobody takes any notice of it. It has survived remarkably well, given the industrial developments which have taken place hereabouts over the last couple of centuries. The rolling landscape of small fields and winding country lanes is dominated by Wingfield Manor itself, an abandoned medieval mansion. Sitting atop an escarpment, Wingfield Manor strikes an evocative silhouette; its ruinous state making it appear all the more romantic. Built in the mid-15th century for Ralph Lord Cromwell, Lord Treasurer to King Henry VI, it was famously used by Bess of Hardwick to keep Mary Queen of Scots under house arrest in 1569 and again from 1584-5 on behalf of Queen Elizabeth I.

There are two history lessons every Derbyshire child learns at school – or at least, there were when I was at school – the plague at Eyam and Mary Queen of Scots being imprisoned at Wingfield Manor. I remember coming on a night hike to 'Wingfield Manor whilst in cub scouts – which freaked me right out. Given the familiarity of the story it is easy to become blasé about Wingfield's claim to fame. However, these events really did have national, if not international significance. 'Imprisoned' perhaps conjures the wrong impression. Mary was kept in comparative luxury (as befitted her royal status), in this and other country mansions by Bess of Hardwick and her husband the Earl of Shrewsbury, at great expense. Rather like a 5-star country house retreat from which you can never leave. Mary, Elizabeth's cousin and rival claimant to the English throne, was the wife of the King of France - Francis II until his death in 1560, and was supported by Philip II of Spain, two of the most powerful men on earth. The French and the Spanish were appalled by England's Protestantism and in the case of Philip, fed up of Francis Drake and his band of legalised pirates plundering his gold ships in the Caribbean and preventing access through the English Channel to the Spanish Netherlands. The two nations pinned their hopes on a Mary-inspired uprising to usurp Elizabeth and reinstate a Catholic monarch on the throne. It is quite humbling to think that such an important figure lived in this very building for so many years.

Eventually, after one too many rumours of plots to launch a coup on behalf of Mary (involving Derbyshire's very own Anthony Babington no less) Elizabeth finally lost patience and had Mary killed.

With direct action the only remaining option, Philip launched his famous Armada to set sail for England. Drake's nimble ships and dastardly tactics put paid to most of the Armada with a few stragglers limping home via the north of Scotland (depositing a few sailors to add to the gene pool in Ireland. Descendants to this day are still referred to as the Spanish-Irish). England's prestige on the world stage was assured. A few years later Mary's son James inherited and combined the English and Scottish thrones for the first time and the rest, they say, is history.

Wingfield Manor was worth a separate visit and so it was that Kimberley, the children and I enjoyed a Sunday walk there. Starting out in South Wingfield we walked past a gentle stream, up an escarpment and on to the top, where we picnicked (we can't get them far without the promise of food) and admired the evocative splendour of the ruinous manor house. Carrying on along the footpath a little further to the south we were presented with fantastic, far-reaching views. I could scarcely believe that such views were possible so close to home.

On another occasion, we embarked on a family walk to the hamlet of Dethick, the former seat of Queen Mary's agent provocateur, Anthony Babington. Babington was convicted of plotting the assassination of Elizabeth I and conspiring with Mary Queen of Scots, an alleged crime for which he was hung, drawn and quartered. Mary meanwhile was charged with treason and eventually executed.

We started out in Lea, a charming village of stone cottages clustered around a green, hidden in a small valley behind the better-known Holloway of Florence Nightingale fame. Proceeding into some woodland, down some steps, over a rushing stream and up the other side, we eventually reached Dethick. If Lea is hidden away, Dethick is virtually invisible; this despite it being situated on top of a hill. Strange how the undulating countryside and woodlands in this part of the world can hide places in this way. I understand why Anthony Babington thought he could get away with writing over 100 coded cyphers to Mary.

Today the tiny settlement of Dethick comprises of the Babington's old manor house, an attached farm and a tiny stone church. After passing through Dethick, a pleasant 'stepping back in time' type experience, we continued along empty lanes in the direction of Riber, before looping back down into the valley and into Lea, where we rewarded our efforts with a drink outside the Jug and Glass Inn – a "proper" village pub.

At the heart of the alleged Babington plot was of course, religion. An attempt to restore a Catholic monarch in place of a devoutly protestant one. It is easy to forget how important a role religion played in politics, and the lives of ordinary people, throughout the medieval and early modern periods. I was reminded of this when I visited the site of an old church north of Brackenfield, a little further up the Amber Valley.

Built into a wooded hillside high above the Amber Valley were the abandoned remains of Holy Trinity Church. The walls of a simple stone chapel quietly survive in an isolated, forgotten place, eerily quiet but for the occasional calls of rooks in the surrounding woodland. The panoramic view from the site is doubtless little changed in centuries, save for the expanse of Ogston Reservoir on the valley floor below. Standing beside the old chapel, a 16th century structure but the origins of which date back to 1086, it was hard to imagine the generations of local people whose lives would have revolved around this sacred place. Below the chapel was a spring producing running water, presumably the reason why this steep, isolated location was chosen for a church. Today, the chapel has been quietly left for nature to gradually reclaim.

Apart from being central to the lives of ordinary people, religion was also, in the 16th and 17th centuries, interwoven with political power. Today religion and politics are by and large separate. Then, they were one and the same. This meant that the monarch or government of the day would feel irrevocably threatened by religious dissent and there was no tolerance afforded for different brands of religious practice, whether it be the Catholic "threat" of the late 16th century or conversely, the rise of Protestant puritans in the early 17th century. It was the latter group whose members set sail on the famous Mayflower ship in 1620 headed for the new world, and established the 'Pilgrim Fathers' colony which became so pivotal to the United States foundation story. The Plymouth Rock colony was small and short lived but by the 1640s tens of thousands of English puritan separatists were setting sail and establishing settlements in Massachusetts. The East Midlands, it so happens, was a hotbed of puritanism. John Cotton, for example, a leader of the First Church of Boston, Massachusetts (1633-52), was born in Derby. It is thought provoking to think that a few bold and zealous churchgoers from this part of England kickstarted and set the tone for what became the world's pre-eminent superpower.

Following the River Amber northwards up to near its source, I reach the village of Ashover. Ashover is another one of those wonderfully hidden places, tucked away behind hills, crags and woodlands somewhere between Matlock and Chesterfield. It feels like 'The Shire' in Lord of the Rings, with its Hobbit-like quality. But Ashover is no mere hamlet, it is a village of some size, and with its compact centre complete with a handful of grand stone townhouse style buildings, it was clearly a place of some significance in its day.

Today, Ashover is particularly well endowed with charming pubs, including the Old Poets Corner, the Black Swan and the Crispin Inn. Outside the latter is a fascinating quote recounting an incident during the English Civil War when Royalist soldiers threw the landlord out of his pub and drank all of its ale. The Crispin itself is believed to have been named after the Battle of Agincourt, fought on St Crispin's Day 1416 and involving local benefactor Thomas Babington of Dethick. Those rascals the Babingtons certainly loved to be in the thick of the action. As for Ashover's connection to the civil war, the village was apparently the scene of a confrontation between the Royalists and Parliamentarians, with the latter stealing lead from the church windows to make bullets and the former generally marauding around smashing the place up and getting drunk.

I am always surprised at how little the English Civil War seems to feature in our popular consciousness. There are endless TV shows, books and plays written about the Tudors, for example, but comparatively little attention is given to the Civil War. This despite it being not one, but three wars involving not just England, but Scotland and Ireland as well. And despite it killing 5% of the population – proportionally more than the First World War - and spawning a military dictator in Oliver Cromwell who led the country through its only period of Republicanism from 1649-60. It is perhaps because of this flirtation with Republicanism, something which feels very un-English (so much so that after 11 years of the experiment, the parliament of the day quietly asked the king's son Charles II to return from exile and take the throne, despite cutting off his father, Charles I's head a decade earlier) that the period receives such little coverage. We don't really know what to do with that sort of history. This is very different to France, for example, which is still a republic and therefore unsurprisingly proud of its revolution, despite the unimaginable terror (liberte, egalite, fraternite and all that).

What we English are more comfortable with is the kind of revolution which is carried out in a quiet, orderly fashion by gentlemen. The kind of revolution which took place in 1688, when three noblemen (one of whom was the 4th Earl of Devonshire from nearby Chatsworth) successfully plotted to depose the last Stuart king, James II, and replace him with the Dutch king, William of Orange (thereafter known as 'The Glorious Revolution'). The three conspirators met in an innocuous stone cottage on Whittington Moor, just a few miles north of Ashover. The cottage has been brilliantly preserved and opened as a museum known as Revolution House.

Connecting Ashover and Whittington Moor is East Moor, a sizeable swathe of empty moorland plateau stretching south to north between Matlock and Chesterfield. Like Sherwood Forest in Nottinghamshire, it was once much larger as old maps attest, but still covers a fair chunk of the county (particularly if you include the peripheral areas which are now farmed but still pretty desolate). The moor contains, aside from anything else, the source of the River Amber. I couldn't resist a brief foray. Upon reaching the moor, I was struck by its mysterious quality. Flat, empty, devoid of civilisation. Criss-crossed by a network of arrow straight roads for no apparent reason. No trees or hedges, just a few weather-battered dry-stone walls and purple heather. Perhaps there were wolves up here, or dragons. Perhaps our old friend Dick Turpin was lurking, waiting to jump out on an unsuspecting vehicle. Perhaps there was a secret military base of the kind which doesn't appear on any maps and the Government doesn't want you to know about.

Perhaps it was time I returned to civilisation before my imagination ran away with me.

I followed the Amber Valley southwards again. Past the graceful Ogston Reservoir, where Ellen MacArthur learnt to sail before going on to single handedly circumnavigate the globe. And where, before the reservoir was created, Joseph Wright painted a romantic scene of the River Amber. Upon reaching Wingfield Park, I peeled eastwards, towards the village of Pentrich. There can be no doubting what Pentrich is famous for. The entrance sign proudly informs you. The Pentrich Revolution of 1819 – England's last armed uprising. How curious it is that the good folk of Pentrich - quiet, law abiding, middle class Pentrich - are so proud of the fact that a gang of men from their village once attempted to commit treason that they boast about it on road signs. Well, treason is perhaps too strong a word. They didn't get very far. A few obligatory pub stops, a failed attempt to steal guns from the nearby Butterley Ironworks, and a march towards Nottingham which dissipated upon reaching the outskirts of the town. More of a pub crawl than a putsch. But let's not be flippant; these men were destitute and desperate. They were also organised, having plotted the uprising for weeks in advance. And the punishment for the ring leaders of hanging and transportation to Australia certainly suggested treason – or at least a government wishing to make an example of them.

We have to put this all in to context to properly understand both the crime and the punishment. The Napoleonic wars coming to an end in 1815 had led to high unemployment. A volcanic eruption in Indonesia led to poor harvests from 1816-1819 which in turn meant food shortages and unrest. Meanwhile the British government had been spooked by the French Revolution of the late 18th century and were worried that something similar could happen in the UK. What happened in Pentrich a little over 200 years ago was symptomatic of the pressures and forces affecting the country at that pivotal time in its history, much like the more famous Peterloo Massacre of the same year, where 18 Mancunian protesters were mown down by overzealous soldiers. The ensuing public outcry eventually led to greater representation for the working classes.

Pentrich is an old Chatsworth Estate village, with a smattering of old stone cottages and farms, interspersed with modern houses and an ancient church. It sits atop a hill overlooking the town of Ripley. As I descended the hill towards my home town, I saw it's three tallest buildings creating a striking silhouette – the Town Hall, The Church and the former Co-op department store, once symbols of the town's civic, religious and commercial pride. Not that there is very much of that particular sentiment left amongst its residents these days. In the foreground, at the bottom of the hill, was one landmark Ripley townsfolk should certainly feel proud of – the site of the Butterley Company. For 229 years, from 1790 until it's abrupt closure in 2009, the Butterley Company produced iron and steel products famous the world over, including bridges, railways, ships and monumental buildings. It's roll call included Vauxhall Bridge, HMS Warrier, St. Pancras Station and in more recent years, the Falkirk Wheel and Portsmouth's Spinnaker Tower. Yet despite this illustrious history, nobody really seems to care about the Butterley site, save for a small band of local enthusiasts who have recently set up a heritage trust. Compare this to the Derwent Valley textile mills, which are on UNESCO's World Heritage Site list alongside the Taj Mahal and the Great Pyramids of Giza.

Upon reaching the bottom of the valley I walked onto the hallowed ground. Forlorn and neglected. Nothing but old concrete and rubble. But look a little closer and there is more, so much more. The old blast furnace, still towering over the site. A few surviving stone factory buildings around the perimeter. And far beneath my feet, the Butterley Tunnel, a 2,819 metre long brick structure built to take the Cromford Canal beneath the works in 1794. A vertical shaft and wharf connects the two, notably used to load Butterley produced cannonballs onto barges during the Napoleonic wars. And it doesn't stop on or beneath the factory site itself. Behind me was Butterley Reservoir, constructed to supply water to the canal tunnel, where I was still able to poke around some of the impressive infrastructure devised to facilitate this purpose. Beside the reservoir was the old Butterley station, now part of the Midland Railway heritage line. I headed eastwards past Butterley Hall, where the owners of the factory once lived, past the Butterley owned farms and the old headstocks, a remnant of the firm's many coal mines, and into the Golden Valley, with its early workers housing and finally I reached Ironville, a 'model' village built by the Butterley company. It became clear that this was not so much a company as an industrial empire. But as I say, almost nobody cares. A pity.

Today, Ironville is statistically one of the most economically deprived communities in the area. Its post office was doing a roaring trade in selling lottery tickets to those hoping for a change in fortunes. And yet places like this never seem to be at the front of the queue to receive Heritage Lottery funding. The affluent village of South Wingfield recently received a seven figure Heritage Lottery grant for the restoration of its former railway station. I have no issue with this – those who successfully bid for the money and have subsequently carried out the work have done a marvellous job. I dare say however that considerably more lottery tickets are sold in Ironville than South

Wingfield and that a grant funded heritage project in the former would be far more transformative for the community.

Half a mile up the hill from Ironville is Riddings, a delightful old village hidden in plain sight amongst more mundane urbanisation. It is the last place you would expect to see Derbyshire's only thatch-roofed pub, the Moulders Arms (or Thack to the locals). But that is not it's only point of interest. Much of the village and adjacent park was laid out by James Oakes, owner of the ironworks which saw the village transform in the early 19th century from a small agricultural hamlet to a thriving industrial community. In 1847 Mssr. Oakes noticed a treacle like substance flowing through one of his coal mines. His brother-in-law, scientist Sir Lyon Playfair, identified the substance as petroleum. Playfair's friend James Young managed to distil the substance into paraffin and wow the Royal institution with a candle-burning demonstration. Oakes set up what was probably the world's first oil refineries in his ironworks and Young made a fortune by commercialising a hitherto valueless substance. Just think about how momentous this chain of events proved to be, and what it ultimately led to. The first distillation and commercialisation of petroleum. Planes, trains and automobiles. A global industry. A tiny gulf state acquiring enough money and influence to host a football world cup. And yet, hardly anyone knows this story, let alone celebrates it. Here is another example of a less fashionable part of Derbyshire underselling its industrial heritage in comparison to the Derwent Valley cotton mills. The other commercial use found by Young for Oakes's treacly substance was a new type of lubricant for cotton spinning machines for goodness sake!

I walked back down to Ironville and on to Codnor Park, where the Butterley Company's second enormous forge used to lie, and reached the River Erewash. The walk southwards along the Erewash Valley was surprisingly rural. This was D.H. Lawrence country. 19th century industrial towns and villages superimposed on a rural landscape and then frozen in time. Rather like a downmarket Derwent Valley. To the east of the Erewash is Nottinghamshire and the old mining communities of Eastwood and Brinsley; tell-tale round hills mark where the spoil heaps of coal pits used to lie. Years and years of backbreaking work to haul coal and earth up to the surface leaving its imprint. On the Derbyshire side is Heanor and Langley Mill. Heanor is an old Victorian market town; one of those places which feels like it used to matter. And it did. Precious few people realise for example that it was formerly the home of William and Mary Howitt (notable travel writer and poet respectively) and of Douglas Keen, whose illustrations adorned the covers of hundreds of thousands of Ladybird books. I don't expect there will be many literary tourists coming here or book festivals anytime soon.

Straddling the Erewash just north of Ilkeston is the marvellous Bennerley viaduct, where I returned on another day for a walk with Kimberley and our daughter Annie. The Bennerley viaduct is an enormous Meccano-like wrought iron structure built in 1877 to take trains across the Erewash Valley floodplain. Closed from 1968 until very recently, when a group of local enthusiasts re-opened it as a recreational footbridge, it's huge rusting hulk stood forlorn and neglected: Rather like the neighbouring old industrial towns of Ilkeston, Eastwood and Heanor, it survived as a testament to former glories but struggled to find a role in the modern day. The viaduct stands as a monument to Victorian confidence and engineering brilliance. It's creators, the Great Northern Railway Company, didn't mess about. This was only a branch line serving a few coal mines but the boggy Erewash Valley wasn't going to stand in their way of breaking the monopoly of the rival Midland Railway line. 443metres of lightweight, flexible latticed wrought iron pillars would see to that.

Walking along the top of the viaduct through the crisp cool air, sunlight glinting in the flooded valley below, was an uplifting experience. I felt elevated, literally and metaphorically, from the drab towns either side. The re-opening of the viaduct as a footway has not merely provided a handy cut through, it has given this magnificent structure a new purpose fit for the 21st century, enabling local folk to reconnect with their history, experience their landscape from a new vantage point and feel proud once again. Like a phoenix rising from the ashes, the viaduct needs to be a blue print for Ilkeston and Heanor et al; they need to find a new role and recapture their sense of pride.

Pausing at the centre of the viaduct we gazed out to the north towards a graceful wind turbine and a recognisable bright blue box that is a monument to the modern age – a monument to Swedish flat pack furniture. I wondered how many of the thousands of people who shuffle through its corridors every weekend would rather be enjoying this experience instead. Not too many I suspect, but I know I would.

Carrying on along the Erewash canal I finally reached the centre of Ilkeston with its tired but still handsome looking town centre, I was reminded that although down on their luck, Ilkeston and the other towns hereabouts are still proper communities with shops, town halls, market places, pubs and close family ties (which is more than can be said for some modern, middle class dormitory towns). In short, they have a sense of identity, and it was this sense of identity which rightly or wrongly in the latest of a long line of acts of protest and defiance, led the people of this region to vote for the UK to leave the European Union in 2019. 61% of Erewash voters chose to leave the EU, much higher than the national figure of 52%. The referendum may seem like a distant memory now, but at the time its result was unexpected and seismic. The communities of the Erewash Valley and others like them across the country determined the outcome, much to the derision and astonishment of the political establishment. This essentially is Brexitland. One might expect politicians to gauge the mood in the Erewash constituency a little more closely – it has after all backed the winning party in every government election since 1983.

As we eventually reached the town of Ilkeston, with its formerly grand but now rundown commercial buildings and its market place which has held a charter fair since 1252, I was reminded of the feeling of pride and sense of community which exists in the towns and villages of this part of the world.

CHAPTER 3

Industry and Innovation
The Derwent Valley

*"And now I see with eye serene, the very pulse of the machine.
A being breathing thoughtful breaths, a traveller between life
and death".*

(William Wordsworth, 1807)

The mouth of the River Derwent lies about a mile east of the village of Shardlow, on the Derbyshire/Leicestershire border where the 50 mile long waterway flows into the River Trent. It is hardly the most awe-inspiring geographical feature. The mouth of the Hudson River it is not! But seldom in the course of human history has so modest a river played host to such enterprise and ingenuity with economic and social consequences of global reach. For the combination of the fast-flowing Derwent and its tributaries (which drop quickly in height from the High Peak to the Trent Valley offering a constant and never-ending power source), some brilliant scientists, engineers, inventors and entrepreneurs and a particular point in time when the political and economic conditions were conducive to change, led to new ways of working and living. But more of that later. For now, I explored the village of Shardlow. Itself a product of the ingenuity of the 18th century and that most peculiar of things, an inland port. For when James Brindley's Trent and Mersey Canal was completed in 1777 and connected to the River Trent, Shardlow became one of the country's busiest river ports. Today it survives in a time warp. Still little more than a village in size, it contains old wharfs, warehouses, cottages and a surprising number of pubs, interspersed with narrow boats of various shapes and sizes. As I strolled along the towpath, I encountered people in their gardens, patios and a couple of balconies even, and sitting outside the pub, all looking out over a narrow channel of brown, stagnant water. I am always surprised at how much people clamour to live next to water, even such small amounts of the stuff. Shardlow, unsurprisingly is much sought after. Its old red brick buildings give it a certain character, charm and sense of authenticity which newly built Mercia Marina cannot compete with.

I continued onwards along the River Derwent path until I reached Elvaston Castle Country Park. Originally a manorial estate, Elvaston was opened to the public in 1970 as one of the first country parks in the country. Six decades of local authority ownership has resulted in a municipal feel and general decay as the County Council increasingly struggles to pay for the upkeep-of its myriad of gardens and buildings.

But look a little deeper and one will find a Victorian gothic wonderland. The story goes that the 4th Earl of Harrington and his wife, the former actress Maria Foote, locked themselves away from the London social scene at Elvaston and hired the gardener William Baron to create an insular, mystical garden for their own amusement. Surrounding the gothic castle with its chivalric interiors were evergreen gardens containing theatrical rock formations, Moorish-style follies and a lakeside walk complete with flame throwing displays. Much of this still remains, albeit not the flame throwing, which is a shame as it would certainly add a bit of jeopardy and excitement to the average Sunday stroll. On the day of my visit, the children's playground and circular walk around the lake were busy with families, but the Elizabethan-come-Victorian Gothic castle was empty and closed, and the gardens virtually deserted. A shame. Elvaston needs revitalising. Perhaps it is time to bring back those flame throwers.

I carried on along the riverside path towards Derby, past the economic might of the Rolls Royce aerospace factory. Through the underappreciated green lung of Alvaston Park and the gritty working-class suburb of Alvaston, an abrupt transition into the urban realm. On to Pride Park, now a modern business park and home to Derby County Football Club, but once the site of the largest locomotive manufacturing base in the country. It is difficult to imagine the scale of the works which once existed in this location and for that matter, the far-reaching effect which the railway industry pioneered here in Derby had. Railways quite literally changed the world. They transformed the British Empire from a bunch of plantation islands and coastal trading posts to continental territories. They made possible the rapid and large-scale transit of troops and armaments necessary to facilitate two world wars. They transformed cities from dense, walkable centres into sprawling suburbs. The Roundhouse is all that remains of the old railway works. A novel building devised for turning trains. A wonderful monument to those forgotten endeavours it is too.

I cut across the southern side of the city to see another icon of Derby's place in the history of the transport industries; the original Rolls Royce factory. The handsome brick façade of the old factory has a central art-deco style stone clad entrance where people apparently used to collect their finished motor cars. Inside is a grand, curving staircase beneath an enormous stained-glass window commemorating the Battle of Britain. In the scene an RAF pilot is stood astride the propellers of a Rolls Royce engine fighter plane, and on his shoulders is a large golden eagle. Heroic stuff. What Rolls Royce developed after the war in the form of the jet engine is perhaps even more remarkable. It still boggles my mind to think that something as large as a Boeing aircraft can be lifted from the ground so effortlessly and propelled across the globe; and more often than not it is a Rolls Royce jet engine that makes that possible. If Derby's railway locomotives helped to make the world smaller, its aeroengines connected its populations like never before.

The main frontage buildings of the old factory have been restored by the City Council and re-used as an office complex but the remainder of the site has been left as fallow waste land like a monument to a lost industrial heyday. This proved to be something of a theme as I proceeded through the southern parts of the city. Mile after mile of Coronation Street-style brick terraced houses. Occasional old factory buildings. The site of Derby County's former home the Baseball Ground where I used to come and watch matches with my Dad as a kid. The Royal Crown Derby factory, still going but evidently at a much-reduced rate. Formerly grand but now tired looking Victorian villas along the main thoroughfares, London Road and Osmaston Road. Set just back from "Ossie" Road, behind some depressingly bland Council flats, I found a diamond in the rough. Arboretum Square is a collection of 19 handsome townhouses which wouldn't look out of place in Kensington if it weren't for the abandoned bins and weeds. At the head of the square is an ornate brick and stone colonnade with a central pediment containing a large statue of local cotton mill owner and benefactor Joseph Strutt, who commissioned this grand building, the square, and perhaps most importantly of all, the adjacent Arboretum Park in 1840. I entered the park and had a stroll amongst its mature trees and undulating lawns. The park had a venerable atmosphere. On this warm day, softened by dappled shade and the occasional fountain, I could have been in Paris or Buenos Aires. The Arboretum Park is said to have been the first public park of its kind and inspiration for Central Park in New York.

Derby is a city of firsts. Derby engineer George Sorocold pioneered public water supply systems which helped to provide mass sanitation for the first time in the UK. Derby MP Samuel Plimsoll invented the Plimsoll line which regulated how much cargo could be safely carried in ships and doubtless saved thousands of lives in the process. The world's first league football match took place in Derby in 1888 and given that the Rams took the kick off, a Derby player was the first to kick a ball in such a fixture. Until its unfortunate closure in 2019 Bennetts of Irongate claimed to be the world's oldest department store. And perhaps most revolutionary of all, Derby was home to what is widely considered to have been the world's first factory, The Silk Mill.

As I walked through the endless rows of terraced houses in the Normanton area of Derby, I was struck by how much poorer this part of town remains compared to other sections of the city. I remember learning at school 25 years ago how deprivation indexes such as life expectancy varied enormously between the City's different suburbs. It doesn't seem as though too much has changed. Perhaps it's because Derby is largely a Victorian city, and the Victorians certainly liked to arrange their housing according to social class. Perhaps it's because we as human beings have a great tendency to group together with other people like ourselves. Tribalism you might call it. Don't get me wrong, people in Derby are friendly, they get on with one another and they come together in the city centre, in workplaces and at the football - but there is no denying that many of Derby's suburbs are distinctly different from one another, socially, culturally, economically and ethnically.

As I entered Normanton Road, the vibrant commercial heart of this diverse part of town, my senses were immediately overwhelmed with a riot of sounds, exotic smells, vibrant colour, bustle and a slightly anarchic atmosphere. I realised not only how much different and exciting this place feels compared to the areas of Derby which I usually visit, but also how infrequently I ever venture to this part of town.

And I'm certainly not the only one. Doubtless there are white, middle-class people living in say, Allestree, who are far more likely to have visited the Grand Bazaar in Istanbul than a Turkish Restaurant on Normanton Road. How strange!

Onwards into the city centre. Past the enormous Derbion shopping centre; originally built by international retail giant Westfield as its first UK centre and prototype for its subsequent London malls. It is disproportionately large and shiny for a town of Derby's size and has consequently sucked all of the life and economic activity out of the surrounding streets like a swirling vortex of polished floors and burger restaurants. Don't get me wrong, the inside of the Derbion is impressive if a little soulless, with its designer shops, multi-screen cinema and bowling alley. But it hasn't done much for the rest of the city centre, or its general vibe as a 'crap town'. You know the kind of place I mean. The sort of towns which were celebrated in the book of the same name for their mediocrity, inner ring roads and rubbish pedestrianised streets inhabited by youths who look like members of the band Goldie Looking Chain. I think part of the problem is that Derby has, since 1977, insisted on calling itself a city. This creates a certain level of expectation which is quickly unfulfilled. In a city, you expect a certain amount of street life and cultural activity. Visit Nottingham city centre on a weeknight for example and you will encounter hundreds of people milling around, en route to theatres, bars and restaurants. Visit Derby City centre on the same evening and you will encounter pigeons and McDonalds wrappers. Think of Derby as a market town however, and a whole different level of expectation is created. You appreciate the fact that it is friendly, small enough to walk around and for the most part, fairly safe.

As I reached the bottom of the slightly down at heel shopping precinct that is St Peter's Street and turned past the grand stone facades of Victoria Street, I was reminded that Derby's reputation for provinciality is perhaps about to change. The soaring new Becketwell development of luxury apartments and performance venue, will see residential accommodation and live acts return to the heart of the city after a long absence. This part of Derby might be quiet now but it has so much potential and so much history waiting to be revitalised. As I stood in front of the Becketwell development I could see many of Derby's finest Victorian buildings, including the former Royal Hotel and Athenaeum, the old central post office and the graceful curve of the Strand with its elegant stone facades. Most of the accommodation within these buildings stood empty waiting to be rediscovered. And in the road beneath my feet was the culverted Markeaton Brook. Just imagine if this was uncovered to create an Amsterdam style waterway.

For Derby has so much history: Roman, Saxon, Viking, Georgian and Victorian. It may not be immediately obvious but it is there. Tidy up the bits in between and there is no reason why Derby cannot shed its mediocre image and become a visitor destination. Derby's other great opportunity lies in the fact that it has the River Derwent running through its heart. Not that for most of the 20th century it seemed to take a blind bit of notice of this fact; successive developments choosing to turn their back on the river.

I walked down towards the river, past the elegant Victorian market hall (another gem thankfully undergoing restoration), past the period looking 1930s Council House and on to the riverside path. The basin and weir behind the Council House were graceful if somewhat overshadowed by the raised inner ring road. North of the river there is a forlorn looking piece of land sandwiched between the river and the monolithic ring road known as 'North Riverside'. Earmarked for redevelopment projects for years which have never quite happened, it now seems disjointed and unloved. Look at a late 19th century map however and a very different picture is painted - one of canal docks, wharfs and tightly packed terraced housing. You can almost imagine the hustle and bustle of the dockyards, kids in rags playing by the canal, and thirsty workers drinking in pubs. The Exeter Arms pub survives as a remnant – if only its walls could talk! Beyond Exeter Bridge, a newly built hotel overlooks the river on the site of what was once a grand townhouse known as Exeter House, where Bonnie Prince Charlie famously signed documents to concede the retreat of his invading Jacobite army in 1745. The prince travelled through Derbyshire en route to London, anticipating the people of Derbyshire to be sympathetic to his cause and willing to take arms and join the march south.

A little further along the path the view opened out to reveal Derby's piece de resistance – The Silk Mill. The Derby Silk Mill is a fantastic monument to the industrial age, indeed the modern age. It all started here. No matter that the present building is an early 20th century rebuild. For all that Cromford and the upper Derwent Valley is feted for being the birthplace of the English factory system, the first true factory was here - a full 54 years before Arkwright built his mills at Cromford. Don't get me wrong, the exploits of Arkwright and Strutt were revolutionary - creating not only new technology, but new types of building and new types of communities - but it was here at the Silk Mill that the awesome sight of a large-scale factory was seen for the first time in 1718.

A modern footbridge affords a pleasant view of the famous Silk Mill, a rebuild of the original mill constructed between 1718 and 1721 for John Lombe. Revolutionary in its day for its scale and technology, Daniel Defoe, author of Robinson Crusoe, famously visited Derby in 1720 and stood in awe at the sight of it, as did American founding father Benjamin Franklin. It also benefits from a Hollywood-esque spy story. Italian authorities reputedly sent an assassin to kill John Lombe for industrial espionage, having allegedly stolen silk throwing secrets after a visit to Piedmont. Lombe died suddenly in 1722.

The Silk Mill marks the southern extent of the Derwent Valley Mills World Heritage Site, a series of early textile mills and associated communities which kick started the industrial revolution in the 18th and early 19th centuries, with far reaching consequences. Sometimes in history there is a time and a place where the right ingredients are present to generate something revolutionary. And so it was in the Derwent Valley 250 years ago. A combination of a fast-flowing river and tributaries from which to harness power, wealthy landowners with capital to invest and raw materials to exploit beneath their estates, workers moving to towns looking for labour (their rural landlords having dispensed with their services when they realised it was more profitable to farm sheep), and a burgeoning global trading empire, bringing in cotton for spinning and opening new export markets. But all of this counted for nothing without human ingenuity; without ideas.

Ideas themselves are occasionally responsible for changing the world. Like when Piles and Frich penned a 3-page paper in 1940 proposing a theory for enriching uranium. Or when Karl Marx began theorising about a communist society. There was a remarkable concentration of great minds and revolutionary ideas in Derby in the 18th century for such a provincial town. Derby played host to philosopher and physician Erasmus Darwin; John Flamsteed, the first Astronomer Royal; and clock maker and scientist John Whitehurst. Darwin and Whitehurst were founder members of the Lunar Society, a renowned group of free-thinking scientists and industrialists, and part of the so-called 'Midlands Enlightenment'. The spirit of the age is captured so evocatively by Derby painter Joseph Wright's mastery of light and shade, in particular his most famous painting - 'A Philosopher Lecturing on the Orrery'. As I walked through Derby's historic core – the market place, Irongate, Queen Street, past Joseph Wright's former home and John Whitehurst's abandoned clockworks - I was able to imagine the atmosphere of the age, and the white heat of innovation and change.

At the top of Queen Street I could see the Roman Catholic Church of St Mary's, designed by the Architect Augustus Pugin who was famous for co-designing the Houses of Parliament. With its perpendicular spire the church is a classic example of 19th century gothic revival architecture. The front of the church stands within ten feet of the canyon-like inner ring road, which was carved through central Derby in 1968. The church may have survived – just – but the same could not be said of the medieval St Alkmund's church which was pulled down as part of the works along with most of Bridge Street, one of Derby's oldest streets containing some fine Georgian buildings. St Alkmund's was a site of pilgrimage for centuries. Archaeological excavations during the works revealed buildings dating back to the 8th century. The only clue of its existence that I discovered was a forlorn plaque beside the concrete walls of the ring road which doubtless nobody ever reads, save perhaps for the occasional guest from the hotel next door, milling around having a cigarette.

St Mary's, Pugin's first Parish Church, is an example (albeit a relatively simple one), of the Gothic revival style. Pugin was a committed proponent of the Gothic style, taking inspiration from the medieval Gothic cathedrals and their pointed arches, ribs and buttresses. His book 'The True Principles of Pointed or Christian Architecture' proposed two primary rules of design – firstly that architectural features must be necessary for convenience, construction or propriety, secondly that all ornament should consist of enrichment of the eventual construction of the building. Put simply, ornamentation with structural purpose. Classical architecture by contrast was considered to be deceitful with its stuck-on ornamentation and concealed structural features, and as structurally primitive.

Pugin, like many of his Victorian contemporaries, believed the Gothic style to be the true Christian style and quintessentially English. It is for this reason that Gothic was chosen as the preferred architectural style for the rebuilding of the Palace of Westminster from 1840 after the previous complex was destroyed by fire. Pugin was chosen to design the new palace alongside Charles Barry and was responsible for much of the exquisite detailing in the Houses of Parliament as well as the design for the iconic Elizabeth Tower (Big Ben).

Although Gothic architecture was viewed in the Victorian period as the 'natural style' and is still seen as being quintessentially English (the Palace of Westminster adorns the label of HP Brown Sauce no less!), like most architectural styles its origins were much more widespread. The medieval Gothic cathedrals which inspired the Gothic revival movement were influenced by early Christian and in particular Islamic architecture. The technology of ribs and pointed arches were first seen in the Middle East and in Moorish Spain, eventually reaching England via France and Italy. Like Christianity itself or the spices which make up our favourite condiment, the origins of these most English of architectural styles lies firmly beyond our shores.

Today the perpendicular tower of St. Mary's church stands proud and resolute above the concrete canyon that is the inner ring road. The four-lane highway runs through a concrete lined cutting a few feet from the base of the tower. It inevitably detracts from the setting of the Church - interrupting views, removing its historic context and adding noise and vibration. Thankfully, in more recent years a footbridge has been installed over the road, pleasingly aligned with the south door of the tower and this offers a pleasant vista (if one ignores the road below).

A monument to post-war urban planning, few infrastructure projects could have had more brutal disregard for heritage than Derby's inner ring road. Nearby St Mary's bridge and chapel, one of only a handful of surviving medieval bridge chapels was also spared, but only just - it's setting irreparably altered. St Helen's House, a Georgian townhouse described as the finest of its type outside of London, and the Derby Silk Mill, are all within spitting distance of the road. Ironically the ring road was only completed in 2011 by which time other cities such as Birmingham were embarking on projects to reverse the distorting effects of their own inner ring roads. I am something of a hypocrite of course, having driven along the road hundreds of times, and recognise that it is far easier for us as a society to be sentimental and protective of our built heritage having benefitted from the relative economic growth and prosperity that flowed from such infrastructure projects. The road was nonetheless brutal in its execution and leaves little trace of what existed before.

I continued northwards along the banks of the River Derwent. A symbol of the brute strength and power of the area's industrial past survives in the form of Handyside Bridge, a stout but nevertheless gracious iron bridge, once taking steam engines but now enjoyed by pedestrians. The bridge was constructed by the once nearby Handyside Ironworks, a company responsible for many a famous structure, including Amsterdam central railway station. To the west was Strutt's Park, a pleasant suburb of late 19th/early 20th century houses, some in the arts and craft style, on the site of the original Roman settlement in Derby.

I entered Darley Park, a wonderfully attractive green lung, made more accessible by a recently constructed riverside path. This is classic English parkland from the old Darley Hall, gracefully sweeping down to the river and framed by specimen trees. The hall is long gone but its terrace survives as a café, offering a view back to the cathedral - if only the tower of a recently built hotel didn't jostle for your attention.

On the opposite side of the river was the suburb of Little Chester, so named in recognition of it being the location of Derby's second Roman settlement – Derventio. Remnants of the settlement were recently uncovered in an archaeological dig which preceded the construction of a flood defence wall. The wall was then rather pleasingly built to follow the original perimeter wall of the Roman fort, complete with pillars to mark the entrance and narrow Roman style bricks.

The Evans family who built Darley Hall made their fortune from cotton spinning in the adjacent Darley Abbey Mills. The associated workers community survives to this day as a much sought after London-style 'urban village'. Clusters of former millworkers cottages exist as if in a time capsule. Once a place of overcrowding and hard, gritty lives I'm sure, but today quaint and benign. I wandered amongst the tastefully gentrified three storey cottages, their rough brick walls, quaint little timber windows and well-kept yards oozing character. A remnant of the Cistercians abbey which predated the mill, still exists as a pub at the heart of the village, albeit it was sadly closed at the time of my visit. Over the river the mill complex itself was a hub of activity - creative businesses, studios, a wedding venue, artisan eateries and lots of local people milling about. I wondered whether today's modern industrial complexes would be like this in 250 years.

I continued northwards along the Derwent Valley, through the pleasant suburb of Allestree with its old village core and great swathe of 20th century housing. The rolling hills of Allestree Park were once parkland to Allestree Hall (still standing but currently empty), before becoming a municipal golf course, but have very recently been re-wilded, one of the first city parks in the world to be re-purposed in such a fashion.

Another rung up the social ladder and I reached the affluent village of Quarndon, which has more than its fair share of millionaires. Originally an estate village of nearby Kedleston Hall, Quarndon has a certain charm, but the growing number of flash modern houses with glazed gables is beginning to compete with its rural character. Eaton Bank and Duffield Bank which cling to the eastern valley side, are similarly prosperous, as is of course Duffield. Following the western valley side, I reached the sought after village of Hazelwood, once a farming village and now a scattered collection of large, impressive houses set in very attractive countryside.

Following the western bank further north still and I passed along Chevinside. Here the Midshires Way footpath offers a panoramic view of the former mill town of Belper, from which the huge extent of the Strutt family's influence on the town can really be appreciated. The Strutt's not only built the substantial cotton mills (and those of nearby Milford) but established a sophisticated community for their employees including workers housing, schools, a hospital, swimming baths, allotments, sports clubs and model farms. This was industrial community building on an industrial scale.

Continuing northwards, I picked up the Portway once again and reached the hamlet of Blackbrook. Blackbrook was once home to a young apprentice of Strutt's mills named Samuel Slater. The genius of Strutt's industrial model wasn't lost on young Slater. He famously took the secrets of Strutt's industrial techniques and established a copycat cotton mill in North America. 'Slater the Traitor' as he became known, amassed a fortune and helped to kickstart the American industrial revolution. A century later and the USA was an industrial superpower and the rest as they say, is history. It is amazing to think how ideas can germinate in innocuous places and then spread with such powerful effect. I walked past the old Slater family farm, a humble abode until Samuel's descendants returned in the early 20th century to spend some of the family's fortune building an American style manor house.

The old Portway continues north through increasingly hilly, and rural countryside. The Chatsworth estate still owns much of the land around these parts and this has no doubt contributed to it retaining its traditional charm. The landscape comprised of old stone farm buildings, cottages and windy lanes largely devoid of modern development. Eventually I reached Alport Heights, the highest point for miles around. The hill is slightly disfigured by the communications masts but looking out from the top the views are panoramic and wonderful. A scene of traditional rural England was stretched out before me. Gently rolling hills, patchwork fields, the Derwent Valley one side, the Ecclesbourne Valley on the other and the steam locomotive of the Ecclesbourne Valley Railway chuffing through.

A mile or two up the road but tucked out of sight in a fold between the hills, was the old lead mining town of Wirksworth. Beneath Wirksworth is a labyrinth of old lead mines so ancient and so extensive that no one is quite sure of their full extent. Stories of mine shafts appearing beneath people's kitchen floors are not uncommon. Given that the town is also surrounded by several enormous quarries it is a wonder the place is still standing let alone thriving.

Kimberley and I brought Jack, Toby and Annie to Wirksworth for the annual wizarding day, a bizarre but increasingly popular celebration of wizardry and witchcraft. Along with hundreds of other families we were bused into town on vintage double deckers; all of the kids and even one or two of the adults dressed in wizard gowns and witches hats. We were deposited amongst the throngs to wander between shops and stalls selling trinkets, and community buildings opened up for craft activities. I figured the experience would be a damn sight cheaper than the Warner Brothers Harry Potter complex in London. That was, until, the kids started working their way through the Harry Potter-themed menu at the Heritage Centre Café.

To escape the crowds, we decided to wander a little further afield. We admired the quiet grandeur of the medieval Parish Church tucked away behind the high street. Its circular churchyard is surrounded by an assortment of old houses. The scale and elaborate interior is testament to the town's former lead mining wealth and in particular that of one man, Sir Anthony Gell. Gell also funded in perpetuity the adjacent almshouses which have been housing the poor since 1550, as well as the old grammar school whose elegant stone façade wouldn't look out of place on Horse Guards Parade. On the opposite side of town were the puzzle gardens, a collection of cottages stacked impossibly on top of one another on the valley sides, connected by a web of paths and alleys. The glimpsed views over rooftops were reminiscent of a seaside village.

Wirksworth is a town undergoing a social transformation from a gritty working community to an artist's mecca, exemplified by its annual arts festival. This is great, but doesn't suit everyone. My cousins recently moved out of the town after several decades because it had become, in their words, too 'arty'. It is widely agreed by historians that Wirksworth was the location of a Roman lead mining settlement but nobody seems to know precisely where this was. In an age of fewer and fewer archaeological uncertainties I love that this information is tantalisingly out of reach and still waiting to be uncovered. It is semi mythical, like the fabled city of Atlantis or Shangri-la. Suggestions that the site of the Roman settlement could be under the nearby Carsington Water reservoir (a Roman villa was found during its construction) further add to the Atlantis comparison.

Back on the main road, we carried on down the hill into Cromford itself. We travelled past the stone workers houses as they stepped down the hill. Arkwright built his houses in the same way as his mills - austere and solid - from massive stone blocks. We arrived at the mill complex itself, with all of its post-industrial gentrification. But the frothy coffees and shops selling knick-knacks did not completely dispel the atmosphere of raw, brutal industry. This was ground zero of the industrial story in the Derwent Valley.

There are a few claimants to the title 'birthplace of the industrial revolution'; Ironbridge in Shropshire and Marvel's Mill in Northampton to name two. However what happened in the Derwent Valley in Darley Abbey, Milford, Belper and in particular Cromford was a combination of things that proved to be truly revolutionary. Large working mills of a scale hitherto not seen before, manned by big workforces on round the clock shift patterns and powered by the manipulation of nature. Purpose-built workers communities and social facilities. The importation of cotton from the Americas, and the exportation of finished goods across the world. Of course, there was industry and organised labour before this point in history. We know the Romans and other classical civilisations had pottery and brickmaking and all manner of other industries, and I daresay the Pharaohs of Egypt required a pretty sizable workforce to build the pyramids. But that particular combination proved so efficient and so effective that it soon spread to Lancashire, the rest of the UK, to France, Germany, Russia, America and beyond.

The list of things the industrial revolution has spawned is mind-boggling. Industrial towns for example (look on a map of the UK and the big splodges - the urban conurbations - are nearly all former industrial towns containing mile after mile of terraced housing), the proletariat, trade unions, Marxism, communism, the Russian revolution, Henry Ford, the US as a global superpower, capitalism as the world's dominant economic system, association football as a mass participation sport (taken from the English public school playing fields and exported around the world by the working classes), binge drinking (the British have always been fond of a drink but I can't help feeling the euphoria of coming to the end of a 5 or 6 day working week fuelled the culture of letting off steam in the pub with your mates), working class culture and humour, L.S Lowry, Peter Kay, industrial warfare and the First World War. I'm not trying to suggest that these pioneering little industrial communities in the Derwent Valley caused all of these things, or that Richard Arkwright invented the modern world; that would be pushing it a bit. But I don't think it's too much of a stretch to suggest that there is a direct link back to this little valley at the end of the 18th century and that this was one of the germination points of the modern age.

It is impossible, of course, to talk about the cotton mills of the Derwent Valley without considering the countless enslaved workers who toiled in the Americas to supply their raw material. The slave trade was abolished in the British Empire in 1807 but it took until 1830 for parliament to abolish slavery itself after years of squabbling between abolitionists and vested interests. Compensation of £20 million was paid to slave owners - 40% of national output - a bailout not repeated until the banking crash in 2008. Enslaved workers got nothing, but were often expected as part of the deal to work up to 6 years longer without pay.

Workers in the mills had a fairly miserable existence too, of course. 13 hour shifts, 6 days a week; children starting work at the age of 7. We must be careful not to fall into the trap of judging by the standards of today however. Arkwright did provide solidly built houses and facilities for workers and their families. But how much of this was philanthropy and how much the need to ensure a steady, reliable supply of workers, in particular women and children? Arkwright had a reputation for being a hard businessman, stamping down on any attempts to replicate his ideas - ironic for someone who's most successful invention was a compilation of pre-existing technologies. I do find it odd that he is hero-worshipped - in particular by intelligent liberal types who would find slavery and child labour morally repugnant. A case of selective amnesia perhaps. As with most historical figures, the truth is more complicated. What cannot be denied is the effect of the dramatic changes stimulated by Arkwright's ingenuity and force of will - changes which ultimately rippled across the world and changed the lives of those early workers and their descendants immeasurably.

The small interactive museum at Cromford Mills did at least paint something of a balanced picture. I was relieved to see that next to the enormous 'god-like' portrait of Sir Richard Arkwright was an even larger mural depicting the toil of countless women and children on three continents which are central to the story of these mills. Enslaved Africans forcibly transported to the Americas to work on plantations which supplied the mills with raw cotton, local workers who worked tirelessly in appalling conditions without breaks, and Indian weavers whose skills inspired the English textile industry but were then supplanted by its mechanised production and British colonial trading laws which prevented Indian exports but encouraged English imports into India.

The kids were momentarily engaged by the museum, but bemoaned the lack of an adventure playground. I suggested that they were lucky that they did not have to work in these mills, as previous generations of children had done. They did not look amused. We went back outside and they had more fun scrambling amongst the rocks and crags behind the mills.

We ventured northwards along the main road up the steep hill towards Cromford. At the top we peeled off onto the High Peak Trail, a former railway line-come leisure path. The boys loved it up there; more climbing and scrambling. The best thing about being a Dad of boys is that you can get away with doing childish stuff yourself without looking odd. At least, you can until you forget you're not 10 anymore and fall off a rope swing to painful effect (as I managed to do). The views from the trail near Black Rocks were panoramic. Cromford was spread out before us in the valley below. Or Arkwright Town as it should perhaps be known. All that Arkwright created could be seen; his cotton spinning mills, his workers houses, shops where only tokens earnt at the mills could be spent (a canny monopoly), hotel for visiting guests, church, pub, allotments, school. And on higher ground surveying the scene, his grand abode, Rock House, and beyond that, his even grander mansion, completed after his death in a Scottish Baronial style, Willersley Castle.

Cromford was perhaps the first fully fledged industrial community. The blueprint for Manchester, where the cotton mills moved to in the 19th century, and so many other industrial towns thereafter. The purpose of all this infrastructure? Philanthropy? Perhaps in part. Above all, it made good business sense. Arkwright wanted families for his mill, in particular women for the knitting machines and children for running around picking up loose cotton from the factory floor. Hellishly hard work, dangerous, extremely long hours and the children started inconceivably young. The men could stay at home for the heavier work of manning the framework knitting machines in the purpose-built lofts of their houses. Reminds me of the post-covid world; all those workers stuck at home on those loathsome virtual meetings.

Returning on another day to Cromford, this time alone, I travelled up the Via Gellia, a narrow deep ravine enclosing a winding road and tumbling brook. The valley sides are so enveloped with trees that the occasional properties which line the road receive almost no sunlight giving the place an eerie quality despite the regular number of lorries heading to Longcliffe Quarry or motorcyclists out for a joy ride. Spurring off from the Via Gellia was the village of Bonsall, another lead mining settlement as ancient but even less changed than Wirksworth owing to its smaller size and isolated position. The village survives as a time warp of industrial archaeology; remnants of old mineshafts, mills and water channels sit curiously in the gardens of houses like the Pompeii of the industrial revolution.

Given the other worldly and singular quality of Bonsall it wasn't a surprise to learn that it is famous today for an unusually high concentration of UFO sightings and for holding annual hen-racing events in the village pub. Too much exposure to lead is known to have induced madness and in times gone by afflicted miners drank copious amounts of ale in the false belief that the drink was a cure for lead poisoning. The poor buggers must have existed in a permanent state of altered consciousness. Perhaps the lead strewn soil and the potent ales served at the Barley Mow are still having something of an effect today.

I took the footpath heading east out of Bonsall past the enormous crater that is Dene Quarry, which sits incongruously next to Cromford, the jewel in the World Heritage Site's crown, and emerged at the aptly named Upperwood. Upperwood is a jumbled collection of old lead miners cottages perched above the popular tourist village of Matlock Bath, which occupies a picturesque gorge below. It is possible to hear the shrieks of children enjoying the rides at the Gulliver's Kingdom Theme Park which sits directly beneath Upperwood and hear the roar of motorcycle engines reverberating from the valley floor, yet few of Matlock Bath's thousands of visitors ever venture up here. Upperwood has a haphazard charm; rustic cottages arranged sporadically around the single lane which winds down the hill, becoming impossibly narrow in places.

I ventured down into Matlock Bath itself. Matlock Bath became a popular spa resort in the 18th century after the construction of grand hotels exploiting the warm natural spring water. It was dubbed little Switzerland by the Victorians after the arrival of the railways, for its alpine like scenery. Today it exists as an inland seaside village with all the benefits and curses this entails. Visit on a quiet day and the riverside walks and cable cars can be charming. Visit on a bank holiday, weekend or during the annual illuminations and the experience follows a depressingly predictable pattern: Queue for 20 minutes through the village. Queue for 20 minutes to find a parking space. Queue for another 20 minutes to buy fish and chips. Run out of patience, return to car and repeat in reverse.

From Matlock Bath I followed an impossibly steep path up the eastern valley side to High Tor, a Victorian pleasure ground atop the limestone bluff which dominates the valley below. The masochist in me can't resist attempting to run up steep inclines like this without stopping. Like Chris Froome tackling the Alpe d'Huez (well not quite), the sense of satisfaction and achievement in reaching the top is palpable. In reaching the top of High Tor I was rewarded with lofty views of the Derwent Valley to the south, the town of Matlock to the north and Riber Castle on another hillside to the east. I was just glad that I didn't bring the kids. In this health and safety conscious age, High Tor pleasure grounds seem to contain a remarkable assortment of hazards including ravines, old lead mineshafts and most surprisingly of all, a completely unfenced 300-foot cliff edge above the Matlock Bath gorge.

I carried on along the eastern valley side to Starkholmes – another old lead mining village which appears to have been built on top of a giant blancmange. The lumpy main road, the closest Derbyshire gets to San Francisco, is the ancient Matlock road pre-dating the 18th century A6 in the valley below. The views from Starkholmes were spectacular. The road eventually led to 'old Matlock' – the original part of Matlock town before it's brief boom and rapid expansion as a fashionable resort in the 1890s. Old Matlock comprises of a stone manor house, a delightful church and a Georgian terrace which wouldn't look out of place in Bath.

From old Matlock it was a short trip to Lumsdale Valley, the site of an abandoned community where small-scale industry flourished in the 18th and 19th centuries then just stopped. This little valley perhaps epitomises the Derwent Valley Mills – an industrial hamlet frozen in time, gradually reclaimed by nature rather like an Aztec ruin being reclaimed by the jungle. Old mill races and wheel pits now form waterfalls amongst the ruins of old factories. It was as though the last shift ended and the factories packed up and buggered off to Lancashire, which is pretty accurate in all truth.

The germ of an idea in an innocuous corner of Derbyshire – relocated elsewhere – spawned Cottonopolous in Manchester and countless other industrial towns across the world and left only this. But how wonderful that it was left. And this was by no means the end of the industrial story for Derbyshire either, as we discuss in the next chapter. Where once there was lead and stone, water and cotton, then there was coal and even oil - two commodities which utterly transformed the world we live in and could yet still have a catastrophic impact on its future.

Navigating the river Trent in a canoe

Following in the paddle strokes of Viking invaders

Narrowboats and knickknacks -Mercia Marina

Genteel splendour -Melbourne Hall

Like a crusader castle -Saint Michael and Saint Mary's church, Melbourne

An evocative scene -the remains of Dale Abbey

*Even the Celts thought this place was special -the great Ridge at
Mam Tor, Castleton*

The focal point of a community for centuries, quietly forgotten -Holy Trinity Church Brackenfield

Victorian engineering excellence rediscovered -Bennerley Viaduct

Walkway along the Bennerley Viaduct

Where there's cotton there's brass -Darley Abbey Mills

Where families once toiled -Arkwrights Mills, Cromford.

More glass than wall -Hardwick Hall

Enjoying the ruins -Bolsover Castle

An unloved gem -chesterfield's oldest pub, the Royal Oak

The English country house at its finest - Sudbury Hall.

Nature's beauty enhanced by human beings -Monsal Dale

Leaving a mark on hallowed ground -Kinder Scout

The finest of views – the Vale of Edale from the top of Jacob's Ladder

On top of the world -trig point above the Amber Valley

Going for a walk here is a stupid idea -Holme Moss summit

Into the abyss -searching for Black Hill summit

It's grim up north -the northernmost tip of Derbyshire: Soldiers Lump at Black Hill summit

There's no place like home -at the Derbyshire/Yorkshire border

CHAPTER 4

Black Gold and Broken Dreams
The Derbyshire Coalfields

"Give me your tired, your poor, your huddled masses yearning to breathe free…."
The New Colossus by Emma Lazarus, 1883, as depicted on the Statue of Liberty, New York.)

I stood at the entrance to "Damstead Park", a modern housing development beside the A38 near Alfreton. Rows of smart detached houses with shiny cars parked outside. In front of me was a small patch of grass which inexplicably had not been developed. There is no trace of it now but the reason that this piece of ground had avoided the diggers was that it was the site of an old coal mine shaft. Not unusual in this part of the world you might think, but this coal mine tells a story. In 1850 an 11-year-old boy called Robert Watchorn toiled within its depths, trying to help his family scratch a living and earn himself a brighter future. After earning enough to secure passage to America at the age of 22, Robert emigrated to begin work in the Pittsburgh coalmines, a common destination for Derbyshire miners at the time. Educating himself in the evenings, he was elected President of the Pittsburgh District Miners Union and worked to abolish child labour in Pennsylvania. He then went on to work for the US Immigration Service, as Chief Inspector at the famous Ellis Island immigration centre where thousands of European migrants famously passed as they entered the United States. He later moved into the oil industry where he amassed a fortune, before retiring to California a wealthy man. But Robert Watchorn never forgot his Alfreton roots. Behind me was a small but handsome park, and across the road a red brick church, smart houses of matching style and the Abraham Lincoln Library (now a Masonic Lodge). Collectively known as the Robert Watchorn Memorial and oozing an American style, they were constructed by the Watchorn family in the 1920s in the great man's honour on the site of his original house.

This rags to riches story captures the essence of the social and economic transformation which took place as a consequence of the industrial revolution. Not that the majority of people were able to achieve the kind of meteoric rise that Robert Watchorn did, of course. But through grit and graft over several generations many ordinary people were able to gradually improve their lot through the 19th and early 20th centuries, their descendants having turned up in the emerging industrial towns as penniless migrants. For it was in the north-east Derbyshire coalfields through the 19th and early 20th centuries where those embryonic industrial experiments carried out in the Derwent and Amber Valleys a century earlier were massively upscaled. And along with it there was entrepreneurship, exploitation, endeavour and opportunity. Fuelling all of this expansion: was one key ingredient: Black gold – or to use its proper name – coal. In the 19th century Britain produced 60% of the worlds steel and 50% of its coal. Britain produced more coal per capita than any other nation on earth right up until 1939. And north-east Derbyshire was at the heart of this coal production.

Derbyshire's population was growing at a faster rate than any other county in the 1890s and that is going some, as the decade was one of rapid population expansion nationwide. Fuelling this growth were the burgeoning coal, steel and textile industries, attracting migrant workers and affording existing residents the kind of stable incomes and home environments where the birth rate rocketed and infant mortality fell. Small villages mushroomed into towns. Factories were established, workers housing built, coalpits sunk everywhere. It was akin to the Californian Gold Rush of the 1840s or the Saudi Arabia of today. Wealth may not have been fairly distributed but it was certainly generated in vast quantities. One of the consequences of rapid economic growth based on dirty, polluting industries of course was climate change – said to be the greatest challenge of our age. I personally believe that global inequality is just as important a challenge, but one that as a society we seem to largely ignore. The two issues are inextricably linked of course. History has suggested that the quickest way to tackle poverty is through rapid industrialisation or the exploitation of mineral resources. China lifted 700 million people out of poverty through rapid economic growth in the second half of the 20th century. We in the developed world like to have our cake and eat it. We benefitted from 'dirty' growth but expect developing countries to pursue a greener approach. Perhaps if we opened our eyes to the unequal distribution of wealth across the globe we might stand a better chance of forging a sustainable future.

I wandered up the hill towards the town centre. To my left was the green expanse of Alfreton Park, formerly the seat of the local gentry family the Palmer Morewoods and today, an underappreciated public park. I walked past a stout little ancient stone building where drunks used to be locked up for the night. At the top of the hill to my left was the remnant historic core of pre-industrial Alfreton; a church, an old market place, a few old brick and stone buildings. To my right was the High Street; the commercial and civic centre of the late 19th century boomtown. Just imagine the pace of construction in the 1890s. The Beijing of today. A population explosion; buildings going up everywhere. But not just thrown up, built with a sense of pride and purpose. There are a few towns of this ilk hereabouts; Ripley, Heanor, Ilkeston, Eastwood; Chesterfield even. Like all gold rush towns, they have since suffered decline. Look past the garish kebab shop fascia boards and neon signs however and you will see smart commercial buildings with grand architectural detailing. Look past the plastic windows and satellite dishes and you will find solid, durable terraced houses - all waiting to be restored, with the uniformity of materials of any Cotswold village. If only anyone would notice and see the value of what is hidden in plain sight. A little carefully targeted investment – restoring the old shop fronts, de-cluttering the streets, re-establishing the markets – would do wonders, before its too late. These towns have had their heyday. Their lights have shone brightly and then diminished but they retain the physical and social fabric needed to rise again. Town halls, churches, shops, pubs, market squares. Family networks stretching back generations and close-knit friendship groups. Compare this with some modern settlements which comprise of cul-de-sacs of detached houses, neighbours who don't talk to one another and precious little else.

I carried on northwards along the arrow-straight A61 down a big hill and up the other side. Through Shirland and Higham, more 19th century mining villages but with older agricultural cores. Eventually

I reached Clay Cross. If ever there was an example of an industrial boom town which then decayed, this was it. George Stephenson, of railway fame, established the Clay Cross Company in 1840; made a fortune, built houses, schools and churches - you get the idea. Everyone was connected to the company from cradle to grave. And then the furnaces stopped burning; the pit wheels stopped turning. What was left was a community so close knit that it famously rebelled en-masse against rises in Council housing rates in the 1970s, and a disproportionately large but sadly decaying high street.

I carried on eastwards to Tibshelf. Another old farming village – turned mining community. I found an historic core of stone cottages and old farmhouses of the type that if they were in the home counties would be worth a fortune, the scruffy remnants of the mining era, and the obligatory smattering of bland 20th century suburban houses. The village entrance sign proudly proclaimed that Tibshelf was the site of the UKs first inland oil well. Wow, maybe I'd taken a wrong turn and accidentally ended up in Texas. If only those early oil prospectors could have known the eventual consequences of their fledgling industry; cars, aeroplanes, plastic, endless wars, colonisation, global warming. Tibshelf lies at the southern end of the Five Pits Trail which, as the name suggests, connects five former pit sites with off-road walking and cycle trails. The Five Pits Trail in turn feeds into a network of other similar trails, stretching like veins across north-eastern Derbyshire, and still growing. What a wonderful far-sighted initiative; to reclaim the acres of spoiled land for nature and give something back to the hard-working people of these old mining communities; they deserve some tranquillity. I could imagine the next Sebastian Coe coming from these parts with such endless training opportunities.

I returned with the family for a bike ride along the trail. Starting at Tibshelf ponds, a wonderful little oasis, we proceeded through rolling countryside for what felt like 20 miles but was probably around 2. A good time was had by all and not a McDonalds or Costa Coffee in sight. The scars of industry were never too far away but this was attractive countryside. A patchwork quilt of fields and church spires – more like D.H. Lawrence country than the Black Country - and best of all, save for a middle-aged man walking his dog and a youth carrying a boom box, there was no-one around.

Onwards we travelled through the Hardwick Hall estate, which the National Trust has maintained in exemplary condition. Parkland, woodland, lakes and atop an escarpment, two grand stone edifices; the Old Hall and the New Hall. Bess of Hardwick a 16th century female magnate and contemporary of Elizabeth I, built the two houses after amassing a huge fortune marrying and outliving a succession of increasingly powerful and wealthy landowners including William Cavendish and George Talbot, Earl of Shrewsbury. The Old Hall, in a craggy and semi-ruinous condition, is maintained by English Heritage. The New Hall, kept in perfect condition by the National Trust, was the ultimate status symbol and architectural marvel of its day, famous for containing 'more glass than wall'.

After leaving Hardwick I noticed a sign proclaiming that Ault Hucknall Church was a mere half a mile up the road and open to visitors. I sneakily dragged the family up the hill in the direction of the church, for what was the longest half mile I've ever experienced, before we reached the little stone church sitting peacefully at the top. It was closed. I could see from some Saxon-looking detailing in the stonework that this building was properly ancient. Another example of an unassuming parish church sitting there unnoticed for century after century while the world changes around it. It was a shame that the church was closed because the main reason that I wanted to come here was that I had read that 17th century philosopher Thomas Hobbes was buried here. Hobbes was a titan of political and moral theory. He argued that a strong central sovereign authority was necessary because people are fundamentally selfish and unruly. It is hard to imagine that someone so influential is buried in this tiny, innocuous church. The only people who look after this place are probably a couple of little old ladies, maintaining an important monument for the nation, for posterity; rather like the final scene in Dan Brown's 'The DaVinci Code' where a monumental secret is hidden in plain sight at Rosslyn Chapel in Scotland.

Across the valley from Hardwick on another hilltop stands Bolsover Castle, the location of another of our family outings. Originally built as a Norman keep in the 11th century the castle was expanded into an aristocratic residence by the wealthy Cavendish family in the 17th century. In its heyday the castle keep contained grand state apartments, a riding school and 'the little castle', a romantic vision of how a castle should be - including castellations, turrets, cupula and exquisitely decorated rooms. Our boys were initially sceptical about the whole experience until I suggested that they could film a YouTube video of the castle grounds. Their imaginations fired, they were soon foraging around exploring every nook and cranny.

From the western side of the keep we enjoyed a commanding view over the valley. We could clearly see the silhouette of Scarsdale Hall on the horizon – another Cavendish house which survives only as an evocative shell, and Hardwick Halls - old and new. A veritable millionaire's row of its day. Almost as interesting in its own way was the sight of the Bolsover model village at the bottom of the slope. A perfectly planned village built for colliery workers in the 19th century, with rows of brick terraced houses arranged in a geometric pattern, alongside a quintessentially English-looking cricket pitch. A match was underway as we surveyed the scene from above; the tiny white players looked like figures from a miniature village.

Back inside the stable range we studied a series of information displays telling the story of Bolsover's most famous inhabitant, William Cavendish (junior – not the William who was married to Bess of Hardwick). Or at least I studied them - the kids were busy dressing up in daft period costumes. William was apparently a very learned man who wrote plays and practically invented horse dressage. All very impressive, but perhaps more impressive given her gender and time of existence, was William's second wife Margaret Cavendish. At a time when girls, even those of aristocratic birth, didn't receive a formal education, Margaret educated herself into becoming a prolific novelist, poet, playwright and philosopher. She even apparently penned one of the first science fiction novels in English and was the first woman to attend a meeting at The Royal Society. Predictably, there wasn't too much made of Margaret's achievements on the display boards. To give him his dues, the "little castle" which William built, was perfectly formed and exquisitely decorated. A curious combination of chivalric, military inspired architecture and enlightened scientific and artistic displays. Representative perhaps of the changing times William's lifetime spanned, and no doubt influenced by his enforced exile on the continent as a defeated Royalist after the Civil War. There were ceilings festooned with twinkling gold stars, fresco paintings and even a small chamber off one of the bedrooms with naked figures painted on every surface. I could only imagine what he got up to in there.

My next destination was the market town of Chesterfield. Heading towards the town from the east I passed vast swathes of what appeared to be recently reclaimed land. Land formerly given over to heavy industry but now re-purposed. A moonscape of spoil heaps clad with sickly looking trees interspersed with newly-built industrial sheds. The region is clearly reinventing itself. I carried on towards town along the Chesterfield canal, itself earmarked for an ambitious urban regeneration project called Chesterfield Waterside. Comprising of waterside apartments, high tech offices and hotels, the proposal is, according to Chesterfield Borough Council, "the UKs 47th largest urban regeneration project". I wondered whether Chesterfield was ready for the UKs 47th largest urban regeneration project. Fair play for the Council for showing some ambition.

Chesterfield and its environs were heavily industrialised during the 19th century thanks to the likes of our old friend George Stephenson, whose former house sits in a park just outside the town centre and whose statue stands outside the railway station clutching a toy locomotive. All of this industry is gone now leaving tracts of land ripe for regeneration. And at its heart, an old market town still survives. A little battle-scarred and rough around the edges perhaps, but a diamond waiting to be polished surrounded by a sea of opportunity. Chesterfield has a lot going for it in my book. The largest outdoor market in England. The delightful Queens Park. Some distinctive black and white timber buildings reminiscent of Chester, and like York, an area of narrow alleys called The Shambles. In the centre of The Shambles I encountered a gem of a building. A jettied, medieval black and white timber framed building forming one half of the Royal Oak, Chesterfield's oldest public house. A sign in the shape of a knight's shield attached to the gable claimed that the building dated from the 12th century and was formerly a rest house for the Knight's Templar in the years of the holy crusades. If there's any shred of truth in the story, the building should be considered a national treasure, not boarded up and unloved as it was at the time of my visit. Around the corner I found another delightful medieval building, The Peacock coffee lounge. The timber framed exterior, dating from around 1500, was apparently only rediscovered behind a rendered façade in the 1970s and sits atop even earlier medieval buildings.

Chesterfield's most famous landmark of course is its crooked spire. The spire, constructed in 1362 upon the Parish Church of St Mary and All Saints (1234), is twisted 45 degrees and leans by 9 feet. The story goes that a shortage of skilled carpenters following the plague resulted in the spire being constructed of unseasoned timber. The placing of heavy lead tiles then did the rest. Or if you prefer, the unusual shape was according to legend the result of a fight between the devil and a magician. Whatever the reason for its peculiar existence, the crooked spire is one of those accidental landmarks. They tend to be the most appealing. Thousands of tourists flock to Pisa every week to have their photo taken next to its leaning tower. Perhaps Chesterfield could become the Pisa of north-east Derbyshire. It has a similar amount of graffiti and stinking drains. And whereas Pisa has its medieval university, Chesterfield has its college. I saw plenty of students during my visit on their lunch break making a bee-line for Greggs.

In all seriousness, with is historic core and blank canvas hinterland, why couldn't Chesterfield turn itself into a great place to live, work and visit. I'm pretty sure York looked this shabby in the 80s. If only it was prepared to do things differently. Perhaps it could start by banning cars. Chesterfield is like a doughnut – the historic town centre surrounded by ring roads, dual carriageways, vast car parks and car orientated warehouse-style retail parks. An urban environment designed for the motor car, where Victorian factories used to be.

We forget how much the invention of the car has influenced our towns and cities, where and how we live. Just like the railway created "metroland" at the beginning of the 20th century, the motorcar resulted in mass migration to newly built suburbs and for those who could afford it, the countryside. My Grandad used to tell me that there was only one car in his village growing up in the 1920s and 30s and that he and his friends used to play football and cricket in the street. Whereas for my parents' generation, the post war baby boomers, the car was king. Car ownership was the ultimate aspiration; streets were for cars, not people.

It is unrealistic to expect people to give up their cars but in allowing cars to dictate the design of our urban environments we have ended up with less attractive and less healthy places to live. Towns and cities have become ever more spread out to make space for roads, which is worse for its inhabitants and not much fun for drivers either. Let's face it, who enjoys driving through a congested city? And that's not to mention localised air pollution or climate change. We should design our towns and cities around people first, cars second. Places that are conducive to walking, cycling, social interaction, access to nature and recreation.

Of course, many longer journeys are easier by car, but car use even for shorter journeys has become habitual. A quarter of car journeys made in the UK are less than a mile. Just imagine the improvement to air quality in cities if most of these journeys were undertaken on foot or by bicycle. Exercise, fresh air, the chance to interact with other people. There is a health imperative. An ageing and longer living population coupled with rising obesity levels and a mental health epidemic dictate that the National Health Service is unsustainable in its current form, if politicians continue to insist on not raising taxes and reducing immigrant labour. Surely prevention is therefore better than cure. If we create walkable neighbourhoods with access to nature and recreation, the population will be healthier and happier and less dependent on the National Health Service. It is depressing that teenagers from poorer areas are more likely to bet on football than play it, or succumb to the crack cocaine of the 21st century; fast food apps. As I walked around Chesterfield looking at the numerous fast-food take-aways and dubious looking nightclubs clearly geared up to one pastime only – getting leathered – I did wonder where we had gone wrong.

I carried on southward along the ultimate monument to the age of the motor car, the M1 motorway. What a technological wonder it must have seemed in its day. When it first opened my grandparents apparently took a bus tour to marvel at it. Exiting at junction 28 I called at McArthur Glen Designer shopping outlet. The complex is an archetypal American-style out of town mall. It is a monument to consumerism and accessible only by car, save for an occasional bus service. Thomas Hobbes' comments about people being fundamentally selfish were ringing in my ears. Acres and acres of warehousing surround the motorway junction. Many are doubtless there to satisfy our insatiable thirst for online shopping; for buying more and more things in a never-ending quest for fulfilment. Maybe the shopping mall has already had its day. Compared to these monolithic boxes, McArthur Glen was suddenly looking rather quaint. We have the Americans to thank for all of this. Henry Ford not only brought car ownership to the masses but in offering significantly higher wages than his competitors to his production workers in return for long, tedious shifts, he created a nation of consumers and a virtuous economic model we are all still trapped in. Artificial intelligence will determine the next economic age. These warehouses will be operated by robots, not people. We will all be stuck at home browsing Amazon marketplace.

On that depressing note, I decided it was time for somewhere altogether more picturesque and wholesome. A place where the spoils of all that industry in the north-east Derbyshire coalfields have been spent creating an idyllic vision of England. Or at least, the illusion of one. It was time for the green hills of the Derbyshire Dales.

CHAPTER 5

Pride and Privilege
The Derbyshire Dales

"I will not cease from Mental Fight, Nor shall my sword sleep in my hand: Till we have built Jerusalem, In England's green and pleasant Land"

(Poem by William Blake)

I stood on a quiet country lane between Duffield and Kedleston. In the middle of an otherwise ordinary-looking field beside the lane was situated, quite incongruously, a gothic temple. An elaborate, exquisitely decorated stone edifice, just sitting there in a grassy field. A medieval cathedral in miniature. How absurd it is that such a monument should have been built in this place. Mind you, how preposterous it is that George Nathaniel Curzon, whose family were responsible for constructing this building, ruled over 400 million people and an entire subcontinent in his role as Viceroy of India at the turn of the 20th century. Or that he led an army into Tibet. Or had Government House in Calcutta built as a replica of Kedleston Hall.

How preposterous is Kedleston Hall itself? It is not a home at all really, but a showpiece; an expression of taste and sophistication, of order and power. Built from 1759 to the designs of the celebrated architect Robert Adam, the hall has a deceptively wide front elevation consisting of pavilions either side of a Greek temple-style portico, giving the impression of an even larger residence. The grand rooms inside were designed to impress prestigious guests - not for living in. Most notable of these is the marble hall, with its columns and statues resembling a Roman villa, and the Saloon, which is topped by an enormous dome based on the Pantheon in Rome. The surrounding park has all that you might expect of such a place – serpentine lakes, a sweeping driveway and arched stone bridge offering strategic views of the hall, all framed by carefully positioned trees, rolling grasslands and random stone follies. The village which used to exist here before the hall was unsurprisingly relocated elsewhere brick by brick, save for the church. And it doesn't stop there. Beyond the park is the estate. Look carefully and you will see that everything was designed; everything had its place. The Kedleston Hotel for visiting guests, the estate cottages, the carefully arranged farmland. This was the English country house at its apogee. A manifestation and representation of the British ruling elite at a time of supreme confidence and power. Sophisticated ostentation. A veneer of power that seemed so self-assured that no-one dared challenge it. Everyone and everything had its place. An endless quest to improve and shape the landscape. The Derbyshire Dales landscape is the perfect example of this. A way of life, and a way of organising society.

Not content with shaping and organising the English landscape and society, the British ruling classes exported their ideals across the globe in the form of the British Empire. It is incredible to think that the British Empire was at its greatest territorial extent only a century ago. A quarter of the world's land surface and a fifth of its population. It was possible to walk from Cape Town to Rangoon without leaving British controlled territory. The Empire was ruthless and paternalistic in equal measure. Unashamed land grabs and the extraction of riches, alongside the exportation of schools and hospitals. Just as the Curzons obliterated the pre-existing village at Kedleston, but housed their workers and made their farmland more productive. The Derbyshire Dales landscape, and in particular Kedleston, survives as a monument to a certain world order.

Another man synonymous with the British Raj in India was the architect Edwin Lutyens. At a time when the sun was already setting on the British imperial project in India, a mere two decades from the independence and partition of the subcontinent,

Lutyens was designing monumental civic buildings for the capital, Delhi, including the colossal Viceroy's house. These buildings sought to create the impression of order, authority and permanence.

As I left Kedleston behind and travelled westwards along the Ashbourne road, I caught a glimpse of Lutyens gift to Derbyshire. Set behind decorative iron gates was a perfectly formed lodge house and a long, landscaped driveway leading to Ednaston Manor. Lutyens designed Ednaston Manor at around the time of the first world war. As the horrors of industrial warfare were wreaking havoc in continental Europe, Lutyens created an idealised vision of Englishness and above all orderliness here in Derbyshire. Ednaston Manor is designed in an Arts and Crafts-come-Queen Anne style. Arts and Crafts buildings tended to celebrate craftsmanship and harp back to a pre-industrial age. This building did not possess some of the more flamboyant flourishes I had seen on other arts and crafts buildings, but was symmetrical and perfectly formed. It was the architectural equivalent of a cucumber sandwich at an afternoon tea – with the crusts cut off. The English Heritage listing description describes Ednaston Manor as being constructed from "Bedfordshire brick". That says it all really; a little piece of the home counties recreated in the Derbyshire Dales.

I continued along the Ashbourne road. As the road dipped into a valley, I encountered another 'lodge' building, some exotic looking trees and the start of what appeared to be landscaped grounds – tell tale signs of another grand abode. This whole area has been moulded and manicured by the great and the good at one time or another. Few passers-by realise that this was once the easterly entrance to the now demolished Osmaston Manor. I carried on along the main road before eventually turning off down a side road to reach Osmaston village, the picturesque estate village for the manor, and beyond that, Osmaston Park. If Kedleston, alongside Chatsworth, represented the pinnacle of the Derbyshire country house estate in terms of sophistication and ostentation, Osmaston Park was its zenith in terms of sheer scale and ambition. A 3,500 acre landscape created from the proceeds of industry for picturesque effect, and for the status and high society acceptance that a complete country house estate brings to a newly monied family. Much still survives. A picture-perfect estate village complete with chocolate box thatched cottages, church, school, pub, village green, duck pond and cricket pitch. And a perfectly formed dramatic parkland landscape, which reveals itself as one crests the hill at the end of the park drive: a vast body of water in the valley bottom, rolling hills and carefully positioned specimen trees. The whole scene is idyllic and serene. At the periphery of the park is Yeldersley Hall; a country house estate in miniature.

At the centre of the estate, but sadly no longer present, perhaps owing to its unsustainable vastness, was Osmaston Manor. Built by the Wright family from 1845-1849 from the proceeds of their industrial concerns at Butterley, the manor house was 330 feet long by 192 feet high and boasted 70 rooms including an enormous palm house and a 4-acre terrace. The neo-Tudor stone-built pile was pulled down in 1965 after the fortunes of the Wright family waned. An edifice and a way of life intended to represent permanence and timelessness, but which in actuality survived only slightly longer than a single century. Still, the whole exercise has left us with this exquisite landscape. For that, we can be grateful to the Wright family and to all those coal miners and ironsmiths whose sweat and toil help to pay for it.

When successful businessmen from 19th century industrial towns sought to create for themselves a country seat, the consequences were often particularly picturesque. Perhaps it was an attempt to escape all of the grime and smog. Or a desire to create something truly beautiful and overtly traditional, as a counterbalance to the rapidly urbanising world. Or maybe they were trying extra hard to earn the status and respect enjoyed by centuries-old landed families. Whatever the motivation, the phenomenon has left us with some exquisite places and the next stop on my journey, Snelston (just a few miles south-west of Osmaston) was another prime example.

John Harrison, a Derby lawyer whose father founded a local foundry, acquired Snelston in the 1820s and employed prominent London architect L.N. Cottingham to create a romantic gothic wonderland. The hall, like something from a Harry Potter movie where you might have expected to see wizards on broomsticks flying between turrets, was so elaborate as to be unsustainable and like Osmaston Manor was demolished in the 20th century. Still surviving today however is a delightfully landscaped park complete with serpentine lake, sweeping grass banks and specimen trees, walled garden and elaborate entrance gates flanked by a perfectly formed stone church and Tudor style lodge house. I could not think of a more beautiful place to be on a sunny afternoon. Below the park I encountered the estate village, also modelled by Harrison and Cottingham, featuring picture-postcard buildings with Flemish brickwork, Tudor-style chimneys and timber frames, including the old school, inn and post office.

In 1832, whilst John Harrison was attempting to create a more beautiful and virtuous world at Snelston, a former son of the village, Michael Sadler, introduced a bill to the House of Commons seeking to limit the number of hours children could work to 10 per day. Although unsuccessful, he went on to chair a parliamentary committee which interviewed 48 people who had worked in textile factories as children. His report shocked the British public and doubtless contributed to subsequent reforms.

A couple of miles west of Snelston, on the Staffordshire border, I came to the tiny hamlet of Norbury.

Norman churches are comparatively commonplace in the English countryside. Norman castles even. But the number of Norman houses is vanishingly small. Here at Norbury somehow, one has survived. The Old Manor at Norbury is a gem of a place. The National Trust now look after the idyllic ensemble of buildings and gardens, which also includes a stone church, larger brick-built manor house of later construction and box-hedge maze. But it was the 13th century original manor house that I was fascinated with. Simple and comparatively small, it was a stout-looking pitch roofed stone building with a medieval hall at first floor level above a storage floor (a two-storey medieval hall is rare, apparently, and a consequence seemingly of the threat of robbery in more lawless times). The little leaded windows and roof trusses were highly evocative. I could step back in time and imagine the original inhabitants, French-speaking descendants of the Norman invaders, enjoying wealth and prestige but still experiencing tensions as they asserted their control over Anglo-Saxon lands.

Continuing my journey south I passed another rarity – for Derbyshire at least – a timber framed Tudor-mansion house, at Somersal Herbert Hall. A marvellously jumbled, leaning, asymmetrical and jettied house set behind fancy iron gates, it looked as though it belonged in Cheshire not Derbyshire, or perhaps a Tudor period TV drama. As the name suggests the hall was constructed by the FitzHerberts, a prominent Derbyshire family who now reside at Tissington, further north. It quietly exists as a private home in a tiny village that almost nobody ever visits; a monument to a bygone age and the evolution of the English country house.

I decided to end my tour of country houses in the Derbyshire Dales at a particular favourite of mine: Sudbury Hall. Sudbury might not have the setting of some of the other houses – the surrounding terrain is pretty flat and the construction of the A50 dual carriageway and His Majesty's prison has hardly enhanced the scene – but the hall itself is a perfect doll's house of a country pile. Like how you would imagine a child would draw a vision of a country house (a child with a particularly advanced architectural vocabulary). Constructed in the late 17th century, Sudbury Hall has everything you might expect to see in a country house: grand symmetrical facades with stone mullioned windows, fancy brickwork, pediments, ornate chimneys, a central cupola, a grand hall, gallery, ballroom and so on.

These days it also has a museum aimed at children which makes it a pretty good place to visit with the family. And so it was that I visited with Kimberley, the kids and my Mum and Dad.

I knew my Dad would appreciate the workmanship of the brick buildings, as a time-honoured bricklayer. I wondered what he thought of the ostentatious display of wealth and social hierarchy. I've never known anyone to graft as hard as my Dad (except perhaps my Uncle Tony, his long-time workmate). Leaving school at 15 with no qualifications to labour on building sites, Dad was determined to better himself. It was through his hard work, and that of my Mum (an NHS midwife for over 40 years), that me, my brother Pete and my sister Rachel, became the first generation in our family to go to university.

On to the market town of Ashbourne, my final stop in the southern part of the Dales. Ashbourne is a pleasant looking town with some grand old buildings from its Georgian heyday and one or two even older, such as the old grammar school (a Hogwarts-esque row of stone gables) and enormous St. Oswald's Church. Ashbourne is a traditional sort of place that still retains a fairly rigid social hierarchy. There are the well-to-do folk and the farmers in the surrounding countryside, the middle-class types attracted to the town by good schools, and those on more ordinary incomes, who tend to reside in the modern housing estates on the edge of town (rather like Oxford). They all come together of course for Ashbourne's great love – the annual Shrovetide football match. I say football – it's more of a free for all. An ancient, more brutal version of the game which used to be popular in many places including Derby, but only seems to survive in Ashbourne and one or two similar towns. I am convinced that Ashbourne's social mix is a reason for its survival. In an olde-worlde order sort of way, people accept their lot and respect their "superiors", but all share a common pastime – kicking the shit out of each other but then shaking hands afterwards and sharing a pint of beer. Or ten. I can think of countless ex-industrial towns where any attempt to organise two days of lawless sport and mass drinking would lead to absolute carnage.

I'll never forget my first experience of Shrovetide football. Standing on the corner of Church Street and Dig Street with crowds of people squeezed between the ancient buildings covering the modern road surfaces and with no cars in sight, I was transported back in time. But this was no gentle re-enactment. Big blokes were pushing and heaving with great gusto, and if the ball suddenly moved and there was a rush to follow it, I had to make dam sure I wasn't in the way to avoid being crushed by the ensuing stampede.

Speaking of stampedes, the next part of my journey would see me enter the Peak District National Park and head towards Dovedale, the scene of many a stampede on bank holiday weekends. I couldn't wait.

CHAPTER 6

Myths and Majesty
The White Peak

*"If we open our eyes, if we open our minds, if we open our hearts,
we will find that this world is a magical place"*

(Chogyam Trungpa)

The Tissington Trail is a recreational path created from an old railway line stretching from Ashbourne northwards into the Peak District. Part of a wonderful network of off-road walking and cycling trails in the Derbyshire Peak District it eventually connects with the High Peak Trail upon which it is possible to continue further north towards Buxton. A perfect location for a family bike ride. We joined the trail beside a nondescript municipal car park near the centre of Ashbourne before immediately entering a long tunnel. Upon exiting the opposite end of the tunnel, as if emerging from a portal into another world, I could see the Peak District stretched out before me in all its resplendent, majestic glory. I was eager with anticipation. I was finally entering the most challenging and rewarding part of the journey. Rather like the final week of the Tour de France when competing cyclists traditionally enter the Alps, I was excited to have a crack at the hills after spending so much time meandering through the lowlands. The moment reminded me of an episode of 1990s sitcom Rab C. Nesbit, in which Rab left his usual Glasgow council estate haunt and emerged in the highlands of Scotland, before pronouncing "THIS is Scotland". For me, THIS is Derbyshire; the part I'm most proud of and aspire to spend time in.

The very first national parks to be established were actually in the United States, but American national parks are all about natural wilderness. The Peak District, the first national park in the UK, is by contrast very much a man-made landscape. It is the product of centuries of human interaction with the landscape; particularly the southern 'White Peak'. Patchwork fields, stone barns, pretty villages, old quarries, railway bridges, country houses – all draped over a varied and arresting landscape of rolling hills and valleys. It is 'developed' in that sense, but most noticeably compared to surrounding parts of this congested country, it is almost completely devoid of 'modern' development – thanks to 7 decades of restrictive planning policies. This gives the Peak District an 'arrested in time' sort of quality. Nowhere typifies this more than the village of Tissington – our first stop on the trail.

Tissington is an old country estate village – come open air museum. With its stout, medieval-looking stone hall, quaint cottages and picturesque duck pond, tourists flock to the village in the summer months for a frothy coffee in the converted stables and a dose of nostalgia for a vision of England which quite possibly never existed. A couple of miles to the west is the dramatic silhouette of Thorpe Cloud, the first proper hill of the southern peaks, but small enough to be manageable and accessible from the adjacent Dovedale. I'll never forget scrambling up Thorpe Cloud with our eldest son Jack when he was about 6 years old and feeling like we'd scaled an alpine peak. Dovedale is a picturesque little valley carved into the limestone by the babbling and crystal- clear River Dove, with impossibly steep sides overlapping one another to give the kind of backdrop that was favoured by the makers of Russell Crowe's Robin Hood film. God knows how they managed to film there without capturing any tourists. I have been to Dovedale on busy weekends and witnessed the improbable sight of thousands of people funnelled into this remote corner of the Derbyshire landscape, marching along the riverside path nose to tail and queuing to cross the famous stepping stones from either side of the river. Traffic lights might have helped prevent a few near collisions as people attempted to cross simultaneously. The hardier venturing up Thorpe Cloud too, climbing boots, hiking sticks, flip flops and all; a great mass of humanity, like gold prospectors streaming up Jacob's Ladder during the great Klondike goldrush.

Back on the Tissington Trail we climbed higher and higher on to more elevated terrain which the kids didn't thank us for. The reward was far-reaching views across a rolling landscape of drystone walls, sheep and the occasional field barn. Even the barns looked pretty. Functional stone buildings constructed purely for utility, yet looking like they belong and enhancing the landscape. The same could be said of the old railway bridges across which the trail passed. I could see occasional narrow 'strip' fields, and ridge and furrow undulations, evidence of medieval farming from a time long before the national park concept existed, and possibly before anyone thought of this landscape as being necessarily beautiful. I suspect that in those days it was a pretty bleak and provincial place. I'm always curious to understand what it is that constitutes a beautiful landscape. It must be an inherently subjective question, influenced by cultural sensibilities and societal traits. Rather like looking at a painting – different emotional responses are evoked in different people who have been exposed to different cultural influences. I dare say that what somebody who has grown up in England considers to be a beautiful landscape is different to what someone who has grown up in China might prefer. It was once suggested to me that we as human beings have a positive emotional response to panoramic views because our caveman brains are re-assured by being able to see that there are no enemies approaching us for miles around. Makes sense I suppose. But why on earth do I like looking at stone barns? And why do people so admire the enclosed and sometimes claustrophobic Dovedale, even when it resembles Piccadilly Circus?

We finally finished our cycle ride near Hartington, another popular tourist village which has a penchant for selling cheese, despite the village's cheese factory having closed down years ago. At Hartington, we converged with a route known as the 'Peak Pilgrimage', a 39-mile trail through limestone countryside from Ilam in Staffordshire to Eyam, the famous plague village in the Derbyshire Peaks. The route is advertised as a modern-day pilgrimage doubtless because of its tranquillity and the poignancy of its final destination. Eyam is where, during the great plague of 1665, villagers voluntarily isolated themselves with tragic consequences in order to avoid spreading disease to surrounding communities.

In medieval times everyone was expected to undertake a pilgrimage at least once in their lifetime. There were local pilgrimage sites such as St. Alkmund's in Derby and those further afield such as Canterbury and Santiago de Compostela in northern Spain. For a rural peasant it might be the only chance to leave his or her village. An opportunity to seek a cure for an ailment, atone for sins or merely seek adventure. A pilgrimage was as much about the journey as the destination, and a long painful slog on foot was part of the deal. It was apt then that I decided to have a crack at a section of the Peak Pilgrimage route on my own and on foot. Running though, not walking. I'm too impatient to walk long distances. I find running meditational; it clears the mind. Unlike walking where I can be distracted by thoughts and stresses, running requires just enough concentration to occupy the mind, but not too much as to overwhelm it. I particularly enjoy running unfamiliar routes. I am endlessly fascinated by what is around the next bend or over the next hill, and therein lies an internal motivation. The steeper the hill the better. There is solace in suffering. Pushing myself past the point where my body is telling me to give up and reaching the crest of a hill induces a tremendous sense of achievement and a rush of endorphins. There is something simple and pure about digging deep and suffering. Of course, I am all too aware that this 1st world version of suffering – a temporary hardship with the promise of a shower and cold drink at the end – is nothing compared to the genuine suffering endured by generations of people who travelled hereabouts and millions who still travel around the world today – but it somehow offers balance and perspective.

The Peak Pilgrimage route followed the remainder of the Tissington Trail, then a section of the High Peak Trail, before veering off onto footpaths through fields towards the village of Monyash. Although a 'managed' landscape rather than an entirely natural one, the White Peak still possesses drama, awe and tranquillity. In any event, a 'pilgrimage' should be about human interaction with the landscape, appreciating what people have achieved or endured before us.

Approaching the village of Monyash, I could see the tall spire, atop a castellated tower, of St. Leonard's Church. A delightful limestone building, the church is particularly large for such a small village, and dates from around 1100. We take for granted the proliferation of ancient churches across Britain. Non-ecclesiastical buildings of such age are extremely rare, yet there are Norman and medieval churches in towns and villages up and down the country, right under our noses. Granted they have usually been altered and embellished, typically by the Victorians, but nonetheless it is amazing to think that such buildings have endured and been used for the same purposes year after year, century after century through the ages, whilst everything else around them has changed beyond recognition. And to think that with ever dwindling congregations, some of these ancient monuments are being held together by a few pensioners putting coppers in a collection bowl.

In our increasingly secular society, spirituality has become marginalised, despite being fundamental to the human condition for millennia. Like every generation we think that we know best and many fail to see the point of organised religion in the modern age. Putting all religious beliefs aside however, one has to acknowledge the magnitude of Christianity as a cultural phenomenon in western civilisation. Spreading from Palestine, through the Roman Empire and then northern and western Europe at astonishing speed, it became central to how populations were governed and lived their lives for centuries. Even today, the pillars of our modern, secular, western societies - the notion of human rights, the rule of law, the weekly and annual calendar - are essentially Christian rules repackaged.

I continued into Lathkill Dale, which had an almost magical quality to it. A hidden little valley carved out by a babbling, crystal clear river. As tends to be the case with rivers running through limestone, the River Lathkill has a tendency to disappear underground for sections before re-emerging again downstream. Even in this unspoilt place, man has sought to manipulate nature, creating a series of weirs in the 19th century for the breeding of trout. This only adds to the gentle drama of the place, of course.

After a remote and exhaustive slog, I finally reached the other-worldly Chatsworth estate. The perfect opulence of Chatsworth House, glittering with gold after recent renovations, framed by grand sweeping parkland and an enormous gravity-fed fountain, was quite a contrast to the earthiness of the pilgrims route. Rather like an 18th century French peasant reaching the gates of Versailles. Completed in 1708 in the English Baroque style, Chatsworth House with its symmetrical front façade embellished with classical columns and an enormous carved pediment, is the perfect vision of an English stately home. It benefits from a dramatic Peak District setting and enjoys all of the trappings of a proper country pile: attractive gardens, opulent interior packed with expensive paintings, perfect looking estate village (Edensor), vast stable block range and a wider portfolio of land, farms and cottages, recognisable from their distinctive blue doors. When so many country estates have been sold off, subdivided, their houses demolished, institutionalised or given over to the National Trust, Chatsworth goes from strength to strength. And the reason for this, it would appear, is the ability of the estate to make money. Lots of it. As well as renting out many of its cottages as holiday accommodation, running a garden centre and kiddies petting zoo, and welcoming paying guests to the hall and garden, Chatsworth hosts an unrivalled series of lucrative events throughout the year. The annual Christmas market is a perfect example. People are attracted in their thousands. Travelling in from surrounding towns and cities, wearing their best leather boots and Barbour jackets, punters will pay handsomely for the privilege of escaping suburbia and feeling, if only for a day, like they belong amongst the country aristocracy. That deep rooted yearning that explains the success of TV shows like Downton Abbey – to be posh and to be in the countryside.

One family who could certainly be described as being posh and in the countryside are the Manners family of Haddon Hall, situated a few miles west of Chatsworth. So posh in fact, that they were able to retain the country pile unoccupied and unaltered for centuries after choosing Belvoir Castle in Leicestershire as their primary residence from 1640 until the early 20th century. Thank goodness they did, because Haddon Hall survives as a perfect example of a medieval country house, preserved as if in a time warp. Eminent architectural historian Nikolaus Pevsner described Haddon as a 'house of knights and their ladies' and a 'dream castle'. A visit with Kimberley to this 900 year old fairytale house was much enjoyed. The higgledy-piggledy courtyard with its gothic arch and cute little mullioned windows felt genuinely medieval, much unlike most stately homes which even if of the same vintage, were generally rebuilt in Georgian or Victorian times. The place had a "patina" of time, the kind of weather worn look that cannot be artificially created and only exists if something is centuries old. Inside, the Great Hall and Long Gallery with their wood panelling, intricate carvings and antlers stuck to the wall gave a shabby-chic Tudor look which was very atmospheric. The whole place had a mythical quality to it. Even the old estate village rather teasingly only survives as a few lumps and bumps on the ground, yet the 12th century parish church still stands. I felt as though transported back in time. It was difficult to figure out which century I was in.

The Peak District has always had a sense of myth and wonder. Our old friend Thomas Hobbes published a list of seven wonders of the peak in 1636 referencing of course the fabled seven wonders of the ancient world. Perhaps in an attempt to avoid the fundamentally 'selfish' masses spoiling them, he published his list of wonders in Latin but they were translated into English in 1682 by Charles Cotton, which soon gave rise to a domestic version of the European grand tour. The list included Chatsworth, St. Ann's Well in Buxton, the Ebbing and Flowing Well at Tideswell, the 'shimmering mountain' Mam Tor, Poole's Cavern at Buxton, Peak Cavern at Castleton and finally Eldon Hole, which is essentially a flipping deep hole in a field. Hardly the Hanging Gardens of Babylon. I think Hobbes could have chosen better.

We continued on to the market town of Bakewell. I once read that Bakewell was the location of a conference of medieval knights. On this day, having just arrived from Haddon Hall, I could well believe that particular legend. Images of King Arthur and his Round Table came to mind. I have always been easily seduced by tales of chivalry. Medieval noblemen went to great lengths to live their lives according to the 'chivalric code'. Brothership, loyalty, a willingness to fight if called upon but a sense of fair play. The kind of values and sentiments which probably inspired the upper classes in subsequent centuries to build empires, serve in the secret service, and play rugby. Or at least that's the romantic version of chivalry. You might alternatively argue that chivalry was used as a veneer to justify bloodshed, and that like all national identity and foundation myths it has been twisted and misinterpreted to suit other ends.

Bakewell certainly feels like an ancient place. The remnants of a 10th century castle. The graceful stone bridge over the River Wye dating from circa 1300 which, with its pointy arches and buttresses, is frankly reminiscent of crusade-state embattlements or a medieval cathedral. It also feels like a very quintessentially English town. The market place and narrow alleys containing little shops selling knick-knacks. The pointy church spire. Every building made of stone. The cricket pitch and the ducks bobbing up and down on the river pecking at discarded fish and chips. The agricultural centre still selling sheep and cattle on a regular basis. Bakewell, and the Peak District at large, exists in a sort of artificial statis where the clock stopped ticking in 1951 when the National Park was established. The Peak District is on the one hand traditional and conservative, but on the other hand has a planning system so restrictive it makes the former Soviet Union Politburo look laissez-faire. You need planning permission to fart in the Peak District. There is a blanket ban on all new-build housing across the district; the only exception being the occasional new house for a local young person with a proven connection to a particular village, the numbers of which are vanishingly small because there are invariably no young people left, so dominant are wealthy retirees and holiday home owners in the housing market. The net result, as the estate agents windows attest, is ludicrously high property values, which only serve to further skew the demographics.

The best thing about Bakewell in my opinion is the Monsal Trail. Another of the Peak District's several former railway lines turned into foot and cycle paths, it stretches northwards through lovely countryside before tunnelling through the hills and then emerging into the glorious splendour of Monsal Dale. It is quite a thrill cycling into a dark, dank, echoey tunnel before suddenly exiting into a bright, expansive, beautiful valley. Monsal Dale is possibly my favourite beauty spot in the Peaks. In the Peak District tradition, it seems to be enhanced by the enormous man-made structure that is the Monsal viaduct, not diminished by it. I'm so fond of it in fact that I chose it as the location to propose marriage to Kimberley several years ago. Plans are now afoot to reinstate a railway line along the route, linking Matlock and greater Manchester. Unsurprisingly the proposal has divided opinion. If it takes some of the thousands of freight lorries off the Peak District's narrow lanes I'm all in favour of the idea. Mind you, had the railway line already been in place I daresay that popping the question would have been decidedly more dangerous, although only slightly more nerve-racking.

We returned to Monsal Dale but this time with 3 children in tow, and continued the trail further north towards Cressbrook Dale and Millers Dale. As though Monsal Dale were not pretty enough, the collection of narrow steep-sided valleys further up the Wye Valley were impossibly picturesque. The meandering River Wye and its tributaries have cut deep gorges into the surrounding limestone plateau, sprinkled with rocky outcrops and wild flowers. Too steep to be farmed, five of the dales hereabouts are preserved for their geological and botanical interest as the 'Derbyshire Dales National Nature Reserve'.

Nature is being given space to flourish here but in the context of the country as a whole, or even the Peak District, this is pretty small-scale stuff. Efforts are well under way to establish an ecological corridor along the old 'Iron Curtain' in Eastern Europe from the Balkans to Finland, where through a quirk of history the absence of people and agriculture has created a haven for wildlife. If such a corridor can be created across a continent, surely such a feature could be achieved in the UK. Most of the upland plateau surrounding these dales and in the Peak District generally is agriculturally poor and populated by a few sheep. Its retention as pasture, supported by agricultural subsidies, is probably more a consequence of our desire as a nation to retain our patchwork quilt landscape for its cultural value, than for its economic or practical benefit. It could easily be turned over to nature, if we had the will to do it. A 30-metre wide corridor could be set aside from coast to coast, linking existing woodlands and wetlands, and managed for biodiversity and wildlife. Perhaps a footpath and cycle path could be incorporated, at last providing a fully connected national recreational network. We could start with the route put aside for the ill-fated High Speed 2 rail project. If only.

At the amusingly named Water-Cum-Jolly Dale we found the monumental edifice that is Cressbrook Mill. With its grand façade topped with a large triangular pediment and cupula, it looked more like

143

the White House in Washington DC than a Derbyshire mill, but conditions within the mill during its heyday were anything but stately or 'jolly'. Cressbrook Mill and Litton Mill a couple of miles upstream are synonymous with tales of child labour and cruelty. Whereas Arkwright's mills at Cromford and Strutt's at Belper attracted 'free' labour, the rural isolation of Cressbrook and Litton meant that their owners had to resort to more nefarious means to secure a workforce. At Litton, orphaned children from London were 'indentured' to man the machines for several years at a time. Ostensibly a philanthropic apprenticeship. In reality a legal form of slavery. The architectural splendour of Cressbrook Mill, juxtaposed with the brutality which took place within. The light and dark of human endeavour. An apt metaphor, as I reached the end of my journey through the White Peak and prepared to enter the Dark Peak.

CHAPTER 7

Mountains and Moors
The Dark Peak

"I lingered round them under that benign sky; watched the moths fluttering among the heath, and hare-bells, listened to the soft wind breathing through the grass; and wondered how anyone could ever imagine unquiet slumbers for the sleepers in that quiet earth".

(Emily Bronte – Wuthering Heights)

The hidden valleys continue to follow the path of the River Wye towards Buxton, through Chee Dale and Wye Dale. All the while, the elevation climbs and the surrounding hills grow taller. At Buxton, the gentler limestone shapes and valleys meet the harder, gritstone moors and hills of the Dark Peak. According to all conventional wisdom, Buxton shouldn't exist. It is remote, inaccessible and inhospitable. It is enveloped by moors and hills. It rains a lot and snows in May. At over 1000 feet above sea level, (making it the highest market town in England) it has a climate like that of Alaska, as my many trips there to play Sunday league football as a teenager attest. And yet it does exist, and has done so since Roman times, thanks to the assumed medicinal qualities of its spring water. But it doesn't just exist as some nondescript town; it exists in exquisite architectural magnificence like the legendary City of Timbuktu within the Sahara Desert, or 18th century Vienna. It is remote yet incongruously beautiful, thanks largely to the efforts of the 5th Duke of Devonshire, who ploughed profits made from his copper mines into building The Crescent in 1788, a grand and gracious terrace similar to the Royal Crescent in Bath. The enterprise put the town on the map as a fashionable spa resort for the upper classes. The Crescent has been recently restored and exudes quality and exclusivity once again. The Duke also had himself constructed a very fancy stable block in the town which, a century later, the Devonshires to their credit converted into a hospital for the poor and added an enormous dome. The awe-inspiring structure is still said to be the largest unsupported dome in Europe.

We visited Buxton for a family camping trip. Clearly, I'd forgotten about the climate. In an effort to stave off hypothermia we had a good tramp around the town, through the splendid pavilion gardens and its botanical conservatory, past the decorative Opera House and the Old Hall Hotel (said to be the oldest hotel in England) and finally the piece de resistance, The Crescent. I was shocked at the opulence of the grand façade. The boys were more interested in the

Ferrari and Lamborghini parked outside. A scruffy-looking man in a knackered old Fiesta promptly pulled up and started filling jerry cans from the public spring water fountain opposite. Good on him. I love the fact that the same mineral water which people with Ferraris are paying £250 a night to bath in is still available for the masses, for free.

We found Buxton to be a curious combination of high-class sophistication and down to earth blokiness. Impossibly well-spoken artistic types attracted by the Opera House and cultural offerings, and stag parties, drawn by the cheap rooms in the overly large Victorian hotels and 2 for 1s at Wetherspoons. A strange, fairytale place, not like anywhere else.

The following day we decided to venture further into the High Peak and visit another fairytale town. Castleton. We drove north along the A6 before peeling off eastwards towards the Hope Valley, at which point we immediately started to climb some "proper" hills. This was real alpine country and the views were spectacular. The Pennines had started in earnest. Upon dropping down into the Hope Valley we encountered a small but perfectly formed town of limestone cottages, cosy looking pubs and chintzy teashops, rather like a scene from a Christmas card. We had a walk through the pint-sized but picturesque Cave Dale, a narrow ravine from which it was possible to see the romantic ruins of the Norman castle which gave the town its name. Perched dramatically above the ravine it was almost as if the whole ensemble had been deliberately created for artistic effect. The boys couldn't resist scrambling up the steep valley sides for a better view. I couldn't resist scrambling after them. There was another geographical feature I really wanted to climb - as tends to be the case when I visit somewhere which is dominated by a large nearby hill - Mam Tor.

Mam Tor, or 'mother hill', is a hulking lump of a hill towering over Castleton. Half collapsed due to a landslip 3600 years ago (how do geologists know this?), the exposed rock has a tendency to shimmer in the sunlight. After driving up Winnats Pass, a photogenic ribbon of road snaking its way through a limestone gorge, we parked the car and set about tackling the hill. We were immediately confronted by 200 or so steps and a steady procession of walkers. I thought we were ascending at a reasonable pace – our 4 year-old rushing up the steps as fast as her little legs could carry her, desperate to beat her older brothers to the top – but were soon shamed into standing aside to allow a group of elderly but seasoned walkers stream past us at a pace Mo Farah would have been proud of.

Upon reaching the summit as the wind buffeted our faces we were rewarded with a wonderfully panoramic vista. Below us to our right the vast expanse of the Hope Valley, with Castleton nestled toytown-like at the bottom. To our left, the corresponding valley of Edale and beyond that the brooding moorland of Kinder Scout, its even higher peaks shrouded in fog and tempting me with the tantalising promise of further challenges. And in front of us, the Great Ridge with its iconic gritstone slabs stretching out into the distance. The scene was truly spectacular. Not in a Himalayan/Andes or even Alpine sort of way, but certainly not bad for a County in the Midlands. And as tends to be the case with the best views in the Peak District, the man-made features somehow enhanced the scene. The Peak District may not be able to compete with the scale or pristine wilderness of some of the more illustrious national parks overseas, but that combination of arresting landscapes shaped by humans over millennia is quite unique. True, our opinion as to what constitutes an attractive landscape changes over time according to our cultural sensibilities, but there is something timeless about Mam Tor and this is borne out by the fact that as the metal motifs around the summit reminded us, Mam Tor was the site of two Bronze Age burial mounds, proof that the site meant something to people up to 7,000 years ago.

After seeing the huge hulk of the Kinder Scout plateau from Mam Tor cloaked in fog and mystery, I couldn't wait to return to the High Peak in order to climb it. And so it was that I arranged a 'boys adventure' a week and a half before my 40th birthday, to try and conquer the mountain.

I set off from Edale in the direction of the summit together with Dad, my brother Pete, my two boys Jack and Toby, brother-in-law Dan and his lad Charlie. The first couple of miles through the Vale of Edale were perfectly scenic but essentially flat and unexciting. It turned out this was not an appealing combination for three boys aged 9, 10 and 11, particularly as the sun was beating down on us with precious little shade. They fell further and further behind, complaining that they were too tired and hot. Any spare energy was expended picking up sticks, jumping on tree stumps, trying to blow blades of grass and generally getting distracted from the task of moving forwards. I thought we'd never get there. I was simultaneously frustrated and worried that I'd expected too much of them. Mercifully, like an oasis in a desert we eventually walked into a farmyard selling cold drinks and ice cream at Upper Booth. Thank goodness for the 21st century. Refreshed and re-charged, the boys enjoyed a new lease of life and, with a little more cajoling and encouragement, we completed the final mile or so to the base of the Jacobs Ladder ascent. A pebbly stream beneath a picturesque stone bridge cooled them down and renewed their interest, and then we powered up the steep steps of Jacobs Ladder to the top, and on to Kinder Scout. The views from the top were fantastic; less bleak and more dramatic than I expected. At a little over 2,000 feet, Kinder Scout can legitimately call itself a mountain, and although this was hardly the Alps, we felt a remarkable sense of achievement. If there is a finer view in England than that of the Vale of Edale from the top of Jacobs Ladder, I have yet to see it.

Approaching my 40th birthday had left me feeling a little more reflective than usual. The previous 10 years had been a blur. One minute you are in your 20s, feeling young, fit and carefree. In what feels like an instant you are staring down the barrel of middle age, having spent the previous decade changing nappies and trying to progress your career. I am embarrassed to say that I have, on occasion, felt slightly 'trapped' by the responsibilities of parenthood and commitments made at work. I say embarrassed because I am acutely aware of how lucky I am to have a young family and genuinely appreciate this every day. I guess it is possible to feel more than one emotion at the same time however, and there has been the odd occasion where I have wanted to get out and do more. But seeing the boys get to the top of Kinder Scout after a hard, hot slog made me feel proud and reminded me that doing this kind of thing with them, whilst challenging, is so much more rewarding than doing it without them. Now they are getting older new joint experiences will present themselves, but at the same time it will not be too many years before they will feel too old and cool to want to spend time with me. I felt a similar sentiment about my Dad. Not that he's old and cool, but that I was glad I could share this with him. A lifetime of working on building sites has left him with a bad back which does not always permit such endeavours. We have to make the most of these sorts of adventures while we are all still willing and able. In tune with this sentiment, my brother Pete bought me a Peak District caving experience for my 40th birthday. I think he was actually trying to get me back for taking him canoeing on his birthday. And so it was that the two of us returned to the Hope Valley yet again a few weeks later, with the promise of a guided trip into the subterranean world, something neither of us had ever done before.

After being picked up by our guide Mark in the Castleton Visitor Centre car park and led up the road to the cave entrance, we were invited to don overalls, wellies and a helmet, quite a feat on the hottest day of the year. We were the only two participants on that afternoon's tour, when there would ordinarily be up to 10. The glint in Mark's eye told me that he saw the opportunity to have a bit of fun with us. He grinned and remarked that the cave system could fill up with water really quickly in heavy rain - and that he hoped the thunderstorms that had been forecast didn't arrive while we were down there. I didn't know whether to laugh or be terrified. It certainly added an edge to the experience.

We entered the cave, sweating and slightly apprehensive, and the temperature instantly cooled. Being a party of only three, we progressed at pace. All of my efforts went into trying desperately not to trip over or bang my head, and to keeping up with Mark. After about a kilometre, we were invited to switch off our headlights and fumble our way forwards in the dark for a few metres. I have never known darkness like it. Mark's confidence in us grew and with extra time afforded by our small party size, he threw in a bit of climbing and crawling over boulders, before the ultimate challenge - a tight squeeze on our bellies through an impossibly small channel.

The extent of the cave system was mind boggling and we had barely scratched the surface. Tunnels extended in various directions, up, down and across. It was clear from the evidence before me that where there is soft limestone, there are caves. The gentle trickle of water was endlessly carving and re-shaping the subterranean rock, like veins in a piece of Swiss cheese. Many cave systems haven't been discovered of course. The famous Titan cave near Castleton contains the biggest natural shaft in the UK (twice the size of St. Paul's Cathedral), and yet was only 'discovered' in 1999. It forms part of a 15-mile network of caves. And that is only one of many different systems. Add to that the innumerable abandoned lead mines and coalmines in the county and it is clear that Derbyshire sits atop an incredibly extensive underground world. Mark told us that his biggest passion was uncovering 'new' caves. I can kind of understand the appeal. In this age of Google maps no part of the world cannot be seen in the click of a button, and yet there are miles of undiscovered caves right under our feet.

I normally pride myself on my intuitive sense of direction, but I must confess to having been disoriented on a couple of occasions. I seriously doubt that I would have been able to find my way out alone, if required to do so. That is a strange sensation, having to put your complete trust in a person you have never metbefore, and hoping that he doesn't have any mishaps in the process. When we eventually returned to the surface the comparative heat of the air felt oppressive. I was glad to be out though. I would liken the experience to watching Derby County lose in a Wembley play-off final. Exhilaration mixed with anxiety. A fantastic experience that I'm pleased I undertook, but not one that I'm desperate to repeat.

Edale marks the southernmost tip of the Pennine Way, a 268-mile long trail along the spine of northern England. After crossing Kinder Scout, the trail continues across moorland in the northernmost portion of Derbyshire (and the Midlands) before crossing into Yorkshire. I certainly wasn't going to let a bit of desolate moorland stop me from reaching the top of this county. And so it was that I returned, once again, to finish the job. First of all, the enormous hulk that is Kinder Scout. I approached Kinder Scout on this occasion from the village of Hayfield, just as the fabled 'trespassers' did in 1932. Kinder Scout may be the highest point of the Peak District but it is not a conical peak but a moorland plateau. Like Table Mountain in Cape Town, it stands majestically above Sheffield on one side and Manchester on the other. Two of England's largest urban conurbations separated by empty wilderness. Given this stark juxtaposition it is little wonder perhaps that the moor played host to one of Britain's most iconic cultural clashes; the mass trespass of April 1932.

After centuries of enclosing common land for sheep and profit, the landed elite had by the beginning of the 20th century engineered the ultimate symbol of defiant privilege by turning Kinder Scout into a giant grouse shooting reserve. Frustrated by their lack of access to the countryside for recreation and escape, young workers from the industrial communities of Manchester and Sheffield gathered at the moor in an act of defiance. The subsequent heavy-handed response by the authorities (several were issued jail terms for their civil disobedience), turned public sympathies against the landowners and spawned a wider appreciation for the need for broader public access to the country's wild spaces, leading ultimately to the establishment of the Peak District as the UKs first national park in 1951.

But how far have we come? Kinder Scout is today recognised as open access land but it took until the year 2000 for this to happen, and today 90% of land in the Peak District is still privately owned, much of it by a tiny number of wealthy families. The Peak District still symbolises Britain's class divide and the differences which exist between urban and rural populations. In concept and in principle it was egalitarian, but in practice it is also elitist. The necessary tight planning restrictions prevent any housebuilding, preserving the limited available homes for the wealthy. One might expect to see the occasional wind turbine in these windy upland areas to supply the nearby urban communities with clean energy, but protection of the landscape takes precedence, no matter how many times our politicians tell us that we need to tackle climate change, or wean ourselves off foreign oil and gas imports. Given the majesty of this landscape I'm not suggesting for a moment that it should be developed, but it is worth remembering that we have a choice. The UK has committed itself to achieving net zero by 2050, and with the cost of producing wind energy now lower than that of producing energy from gas, it is surprising in some respects that we have not blanketed our uplands with windmills. Or placed ground source heat pumps in those endless miles of coal shafts, caves and lead mines. Or placed solar panelled coats on all of those sheep.

Food production is another interesting case. Britain was 80% self-sufficient in the 1980s after the post-war productivity drive, yet we now only produce 50% of our own food. 26% of our vegetables come from the Netherlands for goodness sake; a tiny country. We have one of the most fertile climates on the planet but choose to use our land for other purposes, often for cultural reasons. Hydroponics could increase yields fivefold but there are few who want to see England's patchwork quilt landscape covered in polytunnels. The lack of labour is another factor. You only have to look at the medieval ridge and furrow undulations in the Peak District for evidence that crop cultivation is possible given sufficient human resource. What we choose to eat also has a bearing on our relative self-sufficiency. Meat production is land hungry. Eat a little less meat and we would more easily feed ourselves with the land we have available. Steps are however being taken to repurpose the landscape. The National Trust, one of the biggest landowners in the Peak District, has pledged to plant 20 million trees by 2080. Utility companies are 'rewilding' their landholdings. Some would argue that these measures are merely token efforts designed to satisfy metropolitan liberal sensibilities. That sheep farmers, who have managed the land for centuries and in doing so have maintained its dry stone walls, farmhouses and barns and sustained its communities and cultural traditions, are slowly being displaced. A heavy price to pay perhaps. Ironic also, given that their own descendants were the ones who displaced the peasant farmers 300 years prior, following the enclosure acts.

The ascent from Hayfield up onto the Kinder Scout plateau was steep and dramatic. I followed the River Kinder, past the Kinder Reservoir and finally the steep climb up on to the bleak, brooding moor. The view from the top was expansive and spectacular. Lumpy hills stretching into the distance as far as the eye could see, and perched perilously half way up the slope, the severe but slightly menacing body of water of the reservoir. From this lofty ridge, 2000 feet above sea level, the Pennine Way continues its path northwards across elevated moorland.

The next significant man-made feature encountered by the Pennine Way is the infamous Snake Pass. Snake Pass as the name suggests is a serpentine-like road which traverses the Pennines linking Sheffield and Manchester. The route passes over high moors and encompasses blind bends and steep drops. Unsurprisingly it has a reputation for accidents and is typically the first road to be closed during heavy snowfall. A few years ago, it was apparently voted the seventh most dangerous road on earth. This is probably stretching things a little - I'm sure there are plenty of roads in the Andes and Himalayas that are more terrifying - but I can understand the sentiment.

At its eastern end the road begins beside Ladybower Reservoir. Along with the adjoining Derwent and Howden Reservoirs, Ladybower forms a series of man-made lakes in the upper Derwent Valley, embellished with vast stone-clad dam walls, castellated turrets, aqueducts and weird circular sink holes that you certainly wouldn't want to swim into, all set within a wooded, alpine setting. Add to that the mythology surrounding the fact that the reservoirs were used during the Second World War to practice the famous Dambuster's raids (and are regularly the site of a flypast by vintage Lancaster Bombers) and we have a particularly evocative scene. In true Peak District fashion, a functional man-made feature has been integrated into a dramatic landscape setting to maximum picturesque effect (whether intentional or otherwise).

From the reservoirs the road continues westwards through narrow, wooded valleys before opening out onto barren, windswept moorland. It continues to climb before topping out at around 1700 feet, at which point the Pennine Way crosses its path. The road then starts to descend, and here marks perhaps the most spectacular part of the route. Views to the west appear panoramic and never-ending. Hills as far as the eye can see. The road then winds its way down to lower climbs - like a scene from an Alpha Romeo advert in the Dolomites - before reaching the unlikely destination that is the town of Glossop.

After crossing Snake Pass the Pennine Way continues northward across impossibly remote moorland with scary-sounding names such as 'Cold Harbour Moor', 'Bleaklow' and 'The Swamp'. The prospect of such desolation didn't sound too appealing so I took the road instead, heading into Glossop and then north-eastwards into Longdendale, where could be found yet another chain of reservoirs. The Longdendale Reservoirs were quieter and less picturesque than their upper Derwent counterparts, but nonetheless offered expansive and attractive views, and benefitted from a well surfaced cycle trail along an old railway line. The enormous electricity pylons which straddled the valley and the frequent rumble of HGV lorries driving between Sheffield and Manchester created a brutal atmosphere however, as befit the dark hills and moors all around. The Pennine Way crosses the dam wall between two of the reservoirs before continuing its way northwards across the northernmost part of Derbyshire.

Having started this journey with my brother, on a boat on the River Trent, it seemed only appropriate that I bring him along for the final leg. I managed to persuade him to join me on a hike across the moors to Black Hill, at the very tip of Derbyshire.

Not wanting to miss out on such a foolish endeavour, my Dad asked if he could come along for the ride too. The county satisfyingly culminates in a summit of 1909 feet, marked with an obelisk trig point known as 'soldiers lump', which sounds more like an armed forces pension payout. This was to be our final destination. This was properly far north, considering it was still technically situated in the midlands. Further north than Manchester and Sheffield and Berlin and the southern shores of Hudson Bay. According to my Ordnance Survey map, Black Hill was situated in the parish of Tintwistle, which is almost impossible to say without adopting a northern accent. And as we approached in the car towards the starting point of our walk, I could see that the terrain looked stereotypically northern too. Just as the south of England could be imagined as a single scene – a village cricket pitch, a church spire, a gentle meadow – the view before me exemplified my exaggerated preconception of the north: windswept Pennine moors flanked on the far horizon by mill towns. I half expected Sean Bean to wander past wearing a flat cap and walking a whippet.

At first glance this sort of terrain feels like peripheral, marginal, unproductive wasteland of no use to anyone. The moorland that is, not the north of England. But nothing could be further from the truth. The moors have a symbiotic relationship with the towns and cities which lie beyond them and need to be respected and protected. That relationship rather sums up our relationship with our environment more generally. The upland plateaus of the Dark Peak are covered in swathes of peat bog which until relatively recently, were devoid of vegetation and biodiversity, having withstood two centuries of pollution from the surrounding industrial conurbations. They were emitting carbon into the atmosphere, and leaking acid into the watercourses.

Recent conservation projects have demonstrated the immense benefits of restoring healthy moorlands. They provide natural flood alleviation, as the moorland can absorb and hold heavy rainfall like a sponge, rather than running like a torrent into the narrow, concreted river channels of nearby towns and cities. They can capture carbon to help mitigate climate change – peat bogs can apparently hold more carbon than rainforests. They ensure drinking water purity - many of the reservoirs which provide water to Manchester and Sheffield are situated in the Peaks. And last but not least they encourage biodiversity. A mutually beneficial relationship exists between the countryside and urban areas. Between people, and their environment. The moors here illustrate that perfectly. As a society, we seem to have turned the age-old necessity of looking after the environment in which we live into a huge, complicated, politically-charged debate.

Environmentalism appears to be the new religion. Climate change is the rallying cry of activists willing to chain themselves to motorway barriers, whilst others react angrily at the prospect of having their petrol-fuelled way of life threatened by liberal do-gooders. We are obsessed by high tech and incomprehensively expensive solutions to environmental challenges. For me, caring for our environment should be about common-sense, not culture wars. Spending less money, not more. It is simple, it is obvious and it is imperative.

Anyway, back to more immediate concerns. We turned off the A628 by the dam wall of Woodhead Reservoir and headed north into the hills. As we climbed, the atmosphere became increasingly foggy. I started to wonder whether stopping and going for a walk on the desolate moors was a bad idea. We reached the top and pulled into a small potholed parking area next to a battered looking sign which proudly proclaimed "Holme Moss summit, 524m (1719 ft) above sea level". As we stepped out of the car, a fierce cold wind immediately buffeted our faces. In hindsight, February the 1st may not have been the optimum time of year to undertake such a task, particularly after a period of prolonged heavy rainfall. Looking at the map, the walk to the summit of Black Hill looked no distance at all, and I'm sure that in the summer months there are plenty of people who walk this route with no difficulty whatsoever. But staring out across the featureless moor, with no path discernible, the fog rolling in, water everywhere and a keen wind, I started to regret my decision to bring my brother and my dad here on this day. "We could always leave it, drive back down into Glossop and go for a walk there?" I suggested. Dad was having none of it; "no chance, I'm not driving all this bloody way to turn back now". That was that then.

Off we went, over the wall and into the abyss. The terrain was very tussocky, all heather and bracken, interspersed with standing water. Three steps in and I regretted the decision to not bring waterproof boots. Despite taking great care to step on the vegetation rather than the puddles, every so often my feet would sink into a sodden sponge. Heads down, into the wind we marched. Thankfully the enormous transmitting tower nearby provided a geographical reference point. Picking our way across the waterlogged terrain, the going was ridiculously slow. I looked back after about 20 minutes. Embarrassingly, but also reassuringly, I could still see the car, even in the fog.

Mercifully, a visible path started to emerge. The vegetation worn away to reveal black peat. Things were looking up. I then spotted a vertical shaft-like feature in the distance and felt excited – could this be the trig point which marks the summit of Black Hill already? Like a mirage in the desert, my hopes were dashed when on closer inspection the vertical feature turned out to be a wooden fence post.

On we plodded. There was no-one around save for the occasional grouse that we unwittingly disturbed. But as we approached the top of a valley, I could see a couple of blokes in high visibility coats on the far valley-side planting trees. Reforestation in action. You'd have to be pretty hardy to do their job. Exposed to the valley the wind was ferocious, but the views expansive. I could see the mist rolling around in the valley bottom but thankfully it had lifted somewhat at the top.

We followed the path along the valley top looking for the crossing point marked as 'Ford' on the map. We then passed a grizzled looking hill walker heading in the direction we had come from. I asked him if he knew how far away the summit was. "Five to ten minutes' walk," he proclaimed in a thick South Yorkshire accent. "But the path is very faint, try and follow the stream". Excellent I thought; nearly there. As we rounded the tip of the valley, where the stream which had created it emerged, I spotted in the distance what I was certain was the trig point. Forget following a stream I thought, and led Dad and Pete on a bee-line for the silhouette on the horizon, up and down across the bumpy terrain. After about 15 minutes of very strenuous but increasingly impatient walking, Dad pointed out that the feature I was heading for was in fact a tree. And not just any tree, a frigging Christmas tree. What on earth was that doing there? I suppose the fairy lights and star on top should have been a give-away. Oh dear, that was a stupid mistake. What then followed was 25 minutes of wandering somewhat aimlessly, trying to check my map as it flapped around in the wind and Pete trying to follow Google maps. In the end we opted to follow a stream upwards on the premise that all streams must emerge from a summit. Then, like a phoenix from the flames, the trig point obelisk came into view. I raced towards it, arms aloft, with a feeling of relief and elation. We had made it.

After exchanging a few selfies I stood there for a moment, my feet wet through with freezing cold water and the relentless wind buffeting my face, and briefly reflected. It seemed a long way from where Pete and I had floated down the River Trent in the hazy sunshine at the southern end of Derbyshire. I reckoned that I must have travelled around 500 miles zig zagging across the County. Hardly the most epic of journeys ever undertaken but encompassing vastly contrasting landscapes and thousands of years of history all within the confines of a single county. To crudely paraphrase The Proclaimers – I had travelled 500 miles and I could travel 500 more and I would still have only just scratched the surface. And I'd learnt a valuable life lesson. To never again go wondering across a waterlogged peat bog in midwinter without a spare pair of dry socks.